What Do You See?

André van Zyl

ISBN 0-9740755-1-5

3551 Carriage Glen [illegible]
Dacula, GA 30019
www.gnni.org

Printed in the United States by
Color House Graphics
3505 Eastern Avenue, S.E.
Grand Rapids, MI 49508
www.colorhousegraphics.com

Dedication

I lovingly dedicate this book to:

My Dad, Lambertus Cornelius van Zyl

In 2003 I lost my wonderful father, mentor and friend. I want to dedicate this book to an impressive, stable, uncompromising, loving and caring father. He was a godly man with clear principles that anyone could follow. He has set before me a pathway that will lead me to heaven.

On July 7, my birthday, he departed to his eternal home. Dad, I could never have asked for better. The Lord gave me the best father when He gave me you! I will follow your footsteps, serve Him the way you did, and run the race the way you did. Your baton is now in my hand.

Miss you, Dad!

Acknowledgements

__Naomi van Zyl__ – My covenant partner, greatest friend and lovely wife. You have walked with me through the years, given sacrificially for the sake of the gospel, and traveled thousands of miles to many nations with me. You have excelled in every way, and proven yourself a worthy covenant partner in my life. Your constant faith and steadfastness toward our common goals has strengthened me to pursue my destiny. No one could have done it better! You are an inspiration for life.

__Amoré van Zyl__ – Our only child and daughter. Dad wishes to salute you! You sacrificed your teenage years, those crucial years of a young lady's life, for the sake of the ministry. You paid a great price to leave South Africa to help mom and me establish our family and ministry in the United States. You were uprooted, but your sacrificial attitude impressed your dad and many others. Thank you for understanding my destiny pursuit. You are an irreplaceable blessing, Asjas.

__Pastors Roger and Lori Loomis__ – Thanks for your hard work behind the scenes. You helped to make one of my dreams come true. No one understands more than I do the role you play in our ministry. You were sent by God to us. In and through you, God supplied an incredible blessing. If I can serve others the way you have served me, God will be pleased!

Pastor Steve Huskey -- This talented man has graciously designed the covers for my books. Steve pastors Destiny House Assembly of God in East Liverpool, Ohio. Thank you, friend!

Table of Contents

Foreword

The following men have greatly encouraged me and wonderfully supported this ministry. Each was kind enough to lend his thoughts about this book.

❧❧❧❧❧

From a giant in spiritual stature, with a spirit of humility rarely witnessed in men so greatly used of the Lord, comes an extraordinary compilation of revelatory truth. In his typically insightful style, André van Zyl has boldly defrocked the hidden vestiges of egotism and self-aggrandizement, which so often accompanies those in leadership. In so doing, he courageously charts a new course for men and women of vision to follow, one which is sterling in concept and powerful in application.

Colorfully illustrating these gems of truth by examining the faith and actions of visionaries of old, André powerfully conveys to the reader that there's more to seeing than he ever imagined. As you meditate on the pages that follow, you will glean powerful insights that are desperately needed in order to attain the heightened level of spiritual awareness, integrity, and deportment to which every believer is called.

I have been privileged to call André van Zyl my friend and can say with certainty that his life not only exemplifies the vision and leadership portrayed in this book, but also convinces a person of the need to acquire this understanding. I believe when the message of this book is truly comprehended, there will be an unprecedented awakening of Christians and clergy as they begin to fulfill their divine destiny in the Kingdom.

As you earnestly respond to the question so poignantly posed, "**What Do You See?**" my prayer for you is that the *"eyes of your understanding will be enlightened; that you may know what is the hope of His calling, and the riches of the glory of His inheritance in the saints, and what the exceeding power to us who believe."*

Rodney S. Dukes
Executive Presbyter,
Ohio District Assemblies of God

In one of his books, Stephen Covey includes a picture in which two faces are concealed. One is an elderly lady, the other a young woman. How the picture is viewed determines which person is seen first.

The manner in which an individual looks at circumstances around him determines what he sees. Perspective can be positive or negative, good or bad, hopeful or hopeless. The way his eyes are trained to see will determine what he sees first.

Jesus spoke about this in Matthew 6:22-23, *"The eye is the lamp of the body. So if your eye is sound, your entire body will be full of light. But if your eye is unsound, your whole body will be full of darkness."* Our view on life is determined by the eye we look through!

This is also true when it comes to understanding of the things of God. The way we look at the Word of God determines our own future in the Lord, and our success on earth. Our future depends on what we see. André's writings demonstrate the value of perceiving. This book focuses on what really matters when it comes to our spiritual encounters with God—our real purpose and destiny in this world.

I've known André van Zyl for twenty-seven years, and I can say without a shadow of a doubt, that he personally lives out what he writes about in **What Do You See?** He was, and still is, a man of great vision. He sees beyond the veil and acts with passion on the revelations of God in his life.

My prayer for you is that while you read these chapters, your spiritual eyes will be opened to see as God sees, and not as the carnal person sees. It is time for every servant of God to distinguish between what is real and what is temporary.

See the impossible, and dream how to accomplish it!

Pastor Nico Botha
Executive Board Member, Apostolic Faith Mission
Senior Pastor, Goodwood A.F.M, South Africa

André van Zyl is a man of vision and faith. This book was birthed out of 25 years of revelation from God Himself to André, and André, in turn, revealing God to others. I found my vision sharpened and my faith increased as I read **What Do You See?**

André has ministered in our church more than any other speaker during my 25 years as senior pastor. Why? Because André moves with God! He preaches with power and revelation. He moves in the prophetic with accuracy and grace. Beyond this, he is also a man of great character and faith.

I believe your spiritual eyes will be opened by reading this book. In fact, you may see lots of grapes instead of giants and grasshoppers!

Pastor David Thomas
Victory Christian Center
Lowellville, Ohio

❧❧❧❧❧

The world at large has shifted tremendously toward the supernatural. Sadly, for whatever reasons, the Church has moved away from the supernatural power of God, thus causing a vacuum which the enemy has filled. As we know, one can get all kinds of psychic advice from many sources which run contrary to God's Word.

In this book, André van Zyl speaks clearly about the dangers of such activities, but also gives one a Biblical perspective on how God wants all of His people to operate in the Spirit-realm. Much debate rages in Christian circles about the prophetic gifts and whether these gifts were only for "Bible days."

There are many things about the supernatural that we find difficult to understand with our carnal minds. Nevertheless, this book will help you, in some significant way, to "see" and become a DOER OF GOD'S WILL AND FULFILL YOUR LIFE'S PURPOSE.

Pastors Walter and Colleen Snyman
Lighthouse Rhema Ministries
Cape Town, South Africa

Introduction

If you have 20/20 vision, you have perfect eyesight. Obviously, not everyone is blessed with such wonderful vision. Some are better sighted than others. God has not only given us physical eyes to see, that is, eyes of the flesh, but He has also given us *"eyes of the Spirit."* And He wants us to continually improve our "eyesight".

Why is it so important that we see in the Spirit if we live in the natural realm? The Bible lends support to the fact, that while we live in the physical world, another dimension of reality exists in the spirit world. We are body, soul and spirit. We are both fleshly and spiritual beings. Each of us is allotted a certain number of years to live in our flesh, but our spirit is eternal. Our spirit-man will live forever! The spirit world is so inexplicable and vast that no one can fully comprehend it.

Both light and darkness exist in the spirit realm. We, as believers in Jesus Christ, are people of the light. However, we must cultivate the ability to see in that light. To be an effective follower of Jesus, we must possess the ability to see ahead.

Naturally speaking, blind people need something or someone to lead them. Walking sticks, seeing-eye-dogs, or an arm to grasp are necessary to avoid potential danger. Likewise, it is treacherous to follow someone who pretends he can see, spiritually-speaking, when in fact, he is blind. Jesus referred to them as *"blind guides" (Matthew 23:16).* It is possible to waste years, even decades, following a "blind" leader.

You don't need to be a prophet to see in the Spirit. Nor does the ability to see in the Spirit necessarily qualify you to function in the office of a prophet. All believers are able to "see ahead" because of the indwelling Spirit of God. The Holy Spirit is not a Spirit of darkness; He is Light. The Spirit of Light will never lead you along destructive pathways. Jesus said in John, 16:13, "*When He, the Spirit of truth, is come, He will guide you into all truth: for He shall not speak of himself; but whatever He hears, that shall He speak: and He will show you things to come.*"

In today's stress-filled, uncertain world, growing numbers of people are eager to call psychics to predict their future. Many habitually consult their horoscope. Others visit palm readers. Spiritualism continues to skyrocket, as the universal desire to know about tomorrow surfaces in the spirits of men.

The devil is a copy-cat, always trying to imitate God. Mediums of all types and descriptions have turned man's quest for his future into a multi-billion dollar industry in America. Late-night television features tarot card readers, fortune-tellers and psychic hotlines for those desperate, lonely callers willing to pay accelerated 1-900 fees. The enemy of our soul and our future is willing to do anything that makes him seem like God.

However, only God Almighty knows the future. Jesus, Who is God, is the "Alpha and Omega," the beginning and the end. This title is found in Revelation 22:13, *"I am Alpha and Omega, the beginning and the end, the first and the last."* Our finite mind relates easily to terms like, "beginning" and "end," because we readily understand beginnings and endings. We are born and subsequently die on given dates. We understand the significance of the dash that separates dates on grave markers. Both Genesis 1:1 and John 1:1 start with the phrase, *"In the beginning..."* These Bible writers use this phraseology to give us mortals a time frame. We relate to continuums. Actually, Jesus is "time-less." The only period He was bound by time was the thirty-plus years He walked on earth. He entered time and space as a baby in Bethlehem's manger. But really, He is without beginning or end!

Try to understand that one! You can't; but it is true. Jesus spans eternity past AND eternity future. Somewhere in-between, every human enters into time and space. These introductory words were the Holy Spirit's way of helping us understand the eternality of our matchless Savior! They were employed to assist our limited perspective.

And because He is timeless and eternal, only God knows the beginning from the end. It follows, then, that you can learn more about the future by getting to know God. *"He is the One Who was, and Is, and Is to come" (Revelation 1:8).*

Given this background information, the Bible lays down specific guidelines on how we can see in the Spirit. The Old Testament strictly forbids the consulting of mediums. The Scriptures identify "no trespassing zones," and issue strong warnings to those who press beyond divinely-ordered parameters. Deuteronomy 18:10-12 says, *"There shall not be found among you any one that makes his son or his daughter to pass through the fire, or that uses divination, or an observer of times, or an enchanter, or a witch, Or a charmer, or a consulter with familiar spirits, or a wizard, or a necromancer. For all that do these things are an abomination unto the Lord: and because of these abominations the Lord your God does drive them out from before you."*

You see, the devil uses every one of these detestable mediums to imitate what only God can do. These forbidden practices pervert and destroy God's prophetic plan. The devil is a deceiver. He capitalizes on man's insatiable desire to look into the future and offers him a destructive counterfeit. Ephesians 4:18 tells us that the "god" of this world successfully darkens those who are alienated from the life of God because of the blindness of their hearts. Only born-again people, who have had their blinders" taken off, can see in the Spirit. God "enlightens the eyes of their understanding." The devil successfully propagates confusion in this wonderful arena of Christian living, but God has made it possible for us to "see in the Spirit!"

Perhaps this is why so many believers today shy away from talk on the prophetic ministry. It is a "seeing" ministry. The prophetic ministry is one of the five-fold ministries discussed in the Bible. It is an important, often misunderstood, ministry in the Church. Every Spirit-filled Christian has the ability to see in the Spirit, and all true Christians, because they are in-dwelled by the Spirit of God, have the ability to discern the spirits that are at work in the world and in the lives of people.

Jesus gave to the Church what some theologians refer to as *"ascending gifts."* Before He ascended into heaven, after His post-resurrection appearances, He gave five gifts to the Church. They are listed in Ephesians 4:11 and 12, *"And He Himself gave some to be apostles, some prophets, some evangelists, and some pastors and teachers, for the equipping of the saints for the work of the ministry, for the edifying of the body of Christ."* This passage does not imply that ordinary believers cannot win souls or disciple believers without being a pastor or an evangelist. The Apostle Paul is referring here to those who are gifted for particular callings. Jesus has placed this wonderful five-fold structure in His Church to effectively take the gospel to the nations. Please understand, the five-fold offices do not represent a "new move of God." They are ministry offices that Jesus placed in His Church to help equip the saints. Jesus still places them today, not men!

But listen carefully. You do not have to be an apostle, prophet, evangelist, pastor or teacher to "see in the Spirit." Once you come to this realization, you will begin to move forward, advancing God's kingdom in power and effectiveness. God wants to open your eyes, so you can behold His wondrous dealings!

The church that refuses to "see in the Spirit," and consequently loses its ability to function in the five-fold ministry, cannot counteract the deceitful manifestations of the devil. Sadly, this is one reason why the world is running after counterfeit experiences. The Church has rendered itself impotent, prophetically speaking. The enemy of our soul gladly seduces those who are disenfranchised by the Church with claims of being able to predict their future. Many times, if nothing else, curiosity-seekers fall prey to these ungodly seductions.

My seeking friend, let the Spirit of the living God come on you. Let Him open the eyes of your understanding. If you "see in the Spirit," people will be drawn to you. You will lead them to Christ! Moving in the Spirit will always direct your path toward Christ. Being led by the Spirit will lift you above the moral filth and decadence of this world.

The true mark of Spirit-led living and ministry is that Jesus is glorified. Do not be afraid of the counterfeits. For the kingdom's sake, cast off the prophetic abuses of the past, and seek the real thing. Do not throw the baby out with the bath water! Do you want to "see" Him? Then seek Him!

--André van Zyl

What Do You See?

In Jeremiah 1:11 God asks the prophet this very important question: "What do you see?" Jeremiah's answer satisfied God. The Holy Spirit challenges us with the same question today, and our answer is very important to God. Saint of God, "what do you see?"

When my wife and I were called into the ministry, we were required to meet with the executive board of our denomination. Like every other couple, we were asked these questions: (1) "How do you know you are called into the ministry?" (2) "How do you see yourself?" And (3) "What is your ministry?"

Our leaders believed that if we were called, we would know it; and what we were able to "see," we could explain. People with acute eyesight, spiritually speaking, are confident people. And lest you misunderstand, it is not your goodness that enables you to see in the Spirit. Rather, you function in the Spirit because of His grace and mercy operating in your life.

Good eyesight allows you to observe what is happening all around you. Paying careful attention allows you to plan ahead much better. Can you imagine yourself becoming blind tomorrow? Life, as you know it today, would drastically change. Your abilities would become greatly restricted. Your blindness would make even simple tasks almost impossible to complete.

To do great exploits for God, which requires having the ability to move in the spirit realm, and to see in the Spirit, is just as impossible! We are the only part of God's creation that moves in both the natural and spiritual realms.

God's question posed to Jeremiah forms the premise for this entire book. He speaks lovingly and directly to the prophet: *"Before I formed you in the womb I knew you; Before you were born I sanctified you; I ordained you a prophet to the nations" (Jeremiah 1:5).* God created Jeremiah, and ordained him to be a prophet. God's destiny for Jeremiah was determined in the womb.

In verse 6 Jeremiah replies, *"Then said I, 'Oh, Lord, God! Behold, I cannot speak for I am a youth."* These are the words of a man who does not believe in himself. Like Jeremiah, we many times refuse to do what God asks, not because we don't have the desire, but because we don't believe we can do it. But God cannot and does not lie! When he told Jeremiah that He was ordained a prophet in his mother's womb, He meant it.

Say what you want about your future; God will not change His mind or plan regarding you. Your Father believes in you!

God specializes in creating something out of nothing. Jeremiah was created to be an instrument of God's glory. And you were, too! The reason Jeremiah got hung up on his "prophetic calling," was because he had a hard time articulating his thoughts. *"Ah, Lord God, I cannot speak!" (1:6)* After all, it really helps if a prophet can speak!

God's expectation of us is to excel in the areas of our greatest weaknesses. He says, *"In your weaknesses, I'll make you strong" (2 Corinthians 12:10).*

The very thing that you feel you'll never be able to do is likely to become the very thing in which He will make you an expert.

The word that God gives you is always in direct correlation to the potential He sees in you.

Many times we as parents foresee events in the lives of our children which they may feel are impossible to attain. Their limited understanding causes them to see things differently. Once they become adults, hopefully they begin to see things through the eyes of an adult. Likewise, God sees us through the eyes of the Holy Spirit. It's no wonder that He saw something in Jeremiah that the prophet was unable to see at the time. When God told Jeremiah that he "formed him, sanctified him, and ordained him," he actually expected Jeremiah to believe in himself. God expected him to see in the Spirit. Like Jeremiah, God created you to operate in both the natural and spiritual worlds.

Jeremiah 1:17 says, *"Do not say I am a youth, For you shall go to all to whom I send you, And whatever I command you, you shall speak."*

God would not allow Jeremiah to confess what was not true. As an act of faith, He wants us to agree with Him concerning ourselves. God says to Jeremiah, "Do not say I am a youth. Do not disagree with Me. Do not go against Me. What I command, you will speak."

God does another great thing in verse 9. He touches Jeremiah's mouth. God will touch you at your point of weakness, the place where you need to be strengthened. The touch of God will turn your weaknesses into strengths!

Your abilities come not from your talents, but from His touch.

God also told Jeremiah not to be afraid of the faces of the people to whom he would speak. Eventually, the touch of God on the prophet's life would give him authority to speak to the nations.

Think about it. God chose a youth who stammered, and gave him a national audience! Remember, the reason God did this for Jeremiah, and the reason He will do it for you, is so that when your moment of ministry arrives, you will know that it came not because of your talents or skills, but because of His greatness and grace upon your life.

Never begin your ministry journey following good discussion with God. Wait until He touches you! Only then will you have something to tell, and the ability to tell it with confidence and authority. Do not be like the preacher who stood up and said, "Before I preach, there is something I want to say!"

Where will your message come from? God answers this question in verse 9. He tells Jeremiah, *"I will put my words in your mouth."* It is your mouth, but not your words. That's where faith comes in! Open your mouth and God will fill it. Let the divine intention flow.

Jeremiah's ministry to the nations is outlined in verse 10. God surely placed much confidence in His prophet. He was told to *"root out, pull down, destroy, throw down, build, and to plant."* His was an impressive assignment by anyone's standards! God gave His obedient prophet a word that he was chosen to shake the nations. What a success story!

But wait. Before Jeremiah proceeded with his revelation, God tested him. God challenged his security by asking this all-important question, *"What do you see?"* You can be multi-talented, sing like an angel, and possess a file full of prophetic words spoken over you, but if you cannot see and move in the Spirit, you will not reach the heights God has destined for you. Be encouraged! We were all made in the image of God and have the ability to move in the Spirit.

Jeremiah was called, ordained, and anointed, but he still had to be tested. He had to answer a tough question. A prophetic word spoken over your life does not necessarily mean that you will automatically see in the Spirit. I know people who listen to stacks of prophetic tapes, but they never learn to walk in the Spirit. They never do great exploits for God because they never develop their spiritual eyes.

It is critical that you look into your future through the eyes of the Spirit. If you do, life's storms and difficult decisions will be handled with confidence. Instead of "feeling your way" and making unnecessary mistakes, the eyes of your Spirit will lead you with clarity. Indeed, the future is in God's hands; however, He will share certain things with His seers or prophets. Do you have eyes to see?

Finally, God paid Jeremiah a wonderful compliment in verse 12, *"You have seen well for I am ready to perform my word."* God is ready to perform, but He's waiting on you to get in the Spirit. To be ready, spiritually-speaking, is to have everything and everybody in place. In short, it is to be "strategically placed."

I once read this quote: *"Vision is not mere ideas of the mind, but real pictures of the eyes."* The pictures you see in the Spirit are prophetic lenses on your future. This excites me! The things you see in the Spirit should influence the decisions you make today. Your breakthrough is coming!

Elisha Blinds the Enemy

In 2 Kings 6:8-19 we discover the key to Elisha's wonderful ministry. A direct correlation existed between the prophet's power and his ability to see in the spiritual realm.

The story begins with the king of Syria going to war against Israel (verse 8). He tells his servants that his camp will be at *"such and such a place."* Elisha sends a message to the king of Israel telling him not to pass *"such and such a place,"* as the Syrians were close by. What a wonderful example of someone "seeing in the Spirit!"

In verse 11 we read that the king of Syria suspected that some of his men were spying on behalf of the king of Israel. He was frustrated! One of his servants came forward and told the king of Syria that none of his men had betrayed him. The servant said, *"None, my lord, O king: but Elisha, the prophet that is in Israel, tells the king of Israel the words that are spoken in your bedchamber" (verse 12)*. God was revealing battle plans, spoken in secret, to the king of Israel through the prophetic eyes of Elisha!

By using our spiritual eyes, we become a threat to the enemy. Elisha exposed the Syrians' destructive plans before they attacked. As a result, Israel was able to fight offensively, instead of defensively. As we learn to see in the Spirit, God will also show us the enemy's strategies.

However, being powerful in the Spirit makes us a target for the enemy. As chapter 6 unfolds, we read how Elisha dealt with the on-going attacks against him. According to verse 13, spies report to the king of Syria that Elisha is in Dothan.

Understand, the enemy may know your whereabouts, but that does not mean you are doomed. In view of the fact that we are living on earth, and have not yet arrived in heaven, we must not be surprised when we experience clashes with the enemy. Confrontation with our foe does not foreshadow destruction or anything negative. God has provided a means of escape through Jesus Christ. Always remember, a new level means a new devil!

Satan's plan is to destroy believers who pray and move in the Spirit. His strategy is to capture the "Elisha's," kill their prophetic anointing, and quench the Spirit. If successful, he can break the strength and effectiveness of the Church. However, we are given the assurance that we can face such trials and temptations victoriously through the Spirit of the Lord. Moving and seeing in the Spirit always gives us advantage over the enemy.

2 Kings 6:14 says that the king of Syria came by night and surrounded Dothan with his horses and chariots. The King James Version says, *"...they compassed the city about."* The enemy always operates in the sphere of darkness. Many times we are surrounded by foreboding circumstances. Naturally speaking, everything looks hopeless. It appears that the end is near. The enemy strikes fear in our hearts. The servant of Elisha saw the countless horses and chariots and became paralyzed with fear.

The Bible tells us that *"fear brings torment" (I John 4:18).* The enemy capitalizes on this fear factor and employs it as one of his greatest strategies. Elisha's servant brought a negative report to the prophet, but thank God, Elisha was not moved by fear; He was seeing in the Spirit.

Elisha responds to the servant, "*Those who are with us are more than those who are with them" (verse 16).* I would love to have seen the servant's face when Elisha made that startling announcement! What we see in the Spirit will always over-shadow what we see in the flesh. Elisha did not react; he acted.

Fear could have caused him to overlook God's strategy completely, but he chose to look at the problem through the eyes of the Spirit. His actions were based on facts, not fear. Remember, the enemy always paints an exaggerated and darker picture of your situation. He is a liar. Believe the opposite when he tells you something. In actuality, it was the enemies of Israel who were in trouble, not Elisha or his servant.

The prophet's problem was two-fold. His most pressing dilemma was the surrounding armies; however, his traveling companion did not see things the way he saw them. He had allowed fear to cripple him. Those who do not share your vision cannot walk the same road with you. Much time is wasted on those who do not see in the Spirit. Elisha had both an external and an internal problem! No house can ever come into unity if those within do not see the same thing. The servant's natural reaction was fear; Elisha's Spirit-vision produced faith.

Also, fear distorts the facts and blows them out of proportion. The servant's factual assessment was correct. They were surrounded. However, the "real" truth was that the host of heaven's armies greatly outnumbered Syria's ranks.

Your sickness may be a fact, but focusing on

it may produce fear. The truth is that God can heal you.

Why should you focus on the fact if you can focus on the truth?

In verse 17 Elisha prays a significant, but simple prayer for his servant: *"Open his eyes, Lord, that he may see."* The moment God opened the eyes of the servant, the world around him changed. A clear vision of the spirit world made him see a way of escape. Only minutes earlier, he feared for his life.

Note something: Elisha did not ask the Lord for another miracle for his servant. He simply asked the Lord to open up another dimension to him. As long as we walk in the flesh, we will react like Elisha's servant. However, walking in the Spirit will lift us into dimensions in God where we will not require daily miracles. Constant victory will be the outcome, no matter what conditions surround us.

By verse 18 Elisha was ready to pray strategically: *"Smite these people with blindness."* When you see with the eyes of the Spirit, God puts blinders on your enemy. God does this so we need never fear. Blind people may hear someone enter a room, but they cannot throw a punch. When the enemy hears your voice of authority in the Spirit, he becomes disabled and powerless to strike. Hallelujah!

Elisha used the devil's own tactics against him. Recall that the Bible says, *"The god of this world has blinded the eyes of those who believe not." (2 Corinthians 4:4a)* Elisha blinded his enemy because of his ability to function in a higher dimension. Saint of God, you have authority in the heavenly realm. Look at Elisha's non-military strategy: *"And Elisha said unto them, 'This is not the way, neither is this the city: follow me, and I will bring you to the man whom ye seek.' But he led them to Samaria" (verse 19).* After he blinded Israel's enemy, he led them to Samaria by out-smarting them! Elijah played "hide-and-go-seek" with the Syrians! What a powerful illustration of God-given authority. The Syrian army, along with their imposing display of horses and chariots, meekly followed the man of God.

The days of Elisha have returned. Step up your faith and open your spiritual eyes. Instead of allowing the devil to mislead you, turn the tables on him and mislead him! You have been given authority through Jesus Christ. All of this is predicated on this one truth -- Elisha could see in the Spirit. If this ability was intended only for prophets, pastors and evangelists, why would Elisha ask the Lord to open the eyes of his servant? These are the days of Elisha AND his servants!

Ordinary people will see and move in the Spirit. The abilities of the Spirit-life belong to all who are hungry. As you begin to see in the spirit world, God will turn your natural circumstances around. Victory will be yours!

Elisha's story demonstrates the incredible abilities we have been afforded in the Spirit. The authority that God gives produces mighty results. The enemy is a force to be reckoned with; however, we, who are indwelled by God's Spirit, can deal with him in unprecedented ways. To blindfold the enemy may sound outlandish, but we have the authority to deal with him in a manner that will humiliate him and glorify God.

When the eyes of Elisha's servant were opened, he was able to see the horses and chariots of fire. When you see in the Spirit, you too, will behold similar visions. Sometimes, you may have to wait for the manifestations to appear. Ask the servant of another great prophet named Elijah!

Nothing to See?

In I Kings 18:43-45, Elijah is given instructions from God. *"Go up now look toward the sea. So he went up and looked and said, 'There is nothing.' And seven times he said, 'Go again.' Then it came to pass the seventh time, that he said, 'There is a cloud, as small as a man's hand, rising out of the sea!' So he said, 'Go up, say to Ahab, Prepare your chariot, and go down before the rain stops you. Now it happened in the meantime that the sky became black with clouds and wind, and there was a heavy rain.'"*

When the time came for God to do a miracle, Elijah sent his servant to take a look. Israel had not seen rain in quite some time. In verse 41, Elijah says, *"I hear the sound of the abundance of rain."* Many things are heard in the Spirit before they are manifested in the natural realm. We are not only led by what happens in its manifested form, but can act on what we hear in the Spirit even before it comes to pass. That's why Elijah could confidently say to wicked King Ahab, *"Eat and drink."* Saint of God, go ahead and rejoice about what you know to be true, even before it happens.

Remember, the harvest on your faith statement takes more than one declaration.

Initially, the servant gave Elijah a "no rain in the forecast" report.

Elijah sent his servant boy back seven times to look at the sky. Each time he was convinced that he'd heard the voice of God. Not receiving a sign does not mean you heard incorrectly. Going back seven times shows God that your faith is strong despite evidence to the contrary. The world may think you've lost your mind by demonstrating this kind of faith, but when you know that God has truly spoken, you cannot be derailed.

A few years ago, a nationally-known man of God prophesied that the Twin Towers would come down following an attack from the East. Many scoffed at his words; others simply ignored them. History now records a national atrocity, simply dubbed as "9-11." The veracity of that prophetic word is an indisputable fact. Sometimes days, weeks, months and even years pass, and still nothing happens. But rest assured, whatever God speaks, will come to pass. Our God cannot lie. The time has come for believers everywhere to see and to walk in the Spirit. We must remain spiritually informed. Knowing some things ahead of time will give us opportunities to prepare for warfare, and even the blessings of God.

Proverbs 29:19 says, *"Where there is no vision, (no redemptive revelations of God) the people perish."* Our future and spiritual welfare are secure in the fact that God will always have people who see into the future. These prophetic voices will lead His people. Vision, by definition, is related to the future and not the past. Anybody can see the past. On a more personal level, you are living either in the past or launching into your future.

Reading history books and absorbing facts and information about yesteryear is fine for maintaining perspective; but you must not live in your past. Like Paul, you must *"press toward the mark" (Philippians 3:14).* Your future looms ahead of you. Pursue it! The past is known by reading the manuscripts of yesterday. The future can be seen by knowing God.

Philippians 1:6 says, *"...being confident of this very thing, that He who has begun a good work in you will be faithful to complete it until the day of Jesus Christ."* The work that the Holy Spirit begins in us finds completion in the future. The word "good" in this verse suggests "attractiveness and excellence." It also suggests "the production of results." That dream or vision inside of you came from God. Out of it, God plans to bring something great for both you and others.

Any vision from God will benefit other people.

It will attract others, and be a work of excellence.

The Bible reminds us that everything will pass away. Only God is eternal. The writer to the Hebrews declares that *"Jesus is the same yesterday, today and forever" (Hebrews 13:8).* Premised on this glorious fact, if I remain in Him, I carry the confidence that at some point in my future, things will appear much better than what I now see. In Christ, my life can never deteriorate.

Remember, dreams target your future.

You cannot dream about he past and expect to find fulfillment. That's why people who live in their past stay so frustrated.

A dream is always bigger than your mind can

comprehend, and in one sense, unreachable. God's dream through Jeremiah was to reach the nations. This was much too big for Jeremiah. That's why he originally rebelled at the notion.

You see, dreams that are manageable are probably not God-given dreams.

To say that God is big is an understatement. He plans and thinks much bigger than your mind can comprehend. God-given dreams often threaten the receiver! He created us with the ability to think, and so He challenges our comfort zones with dreams. That's why He asked Jeremiah, *"What do you see?"* He was not referring to his physical eyesight, but to the prophet's ability to see in the Spirit.

Subsequently, God says to Jeremiah, *"I am ready to perform my word."* Jeremiah was ready, too! God moves with a man who moves. Go ahead. Challenge such a man, and see if you can scare him off with your dream!

Church leaders who cannot dream or see in the Spirit will produce frustrated followers. When everything comes to an abrupt halt, stagnation moves in. After stagnation comes death. And of course, death makes any future movement impossible.

Philippians 3:12-14 says, *"Not that I have already attained, or I am already perfected; but I press on, that I may lay hold of that for which Christ Jesus has also laid hold of me. Brethren, I do not count myself to have apprehended, but one thing I do, forgetting those things which are behind and reaching forward to those things which are ahead, I press toward the goal for the prize of the upward call of God in Christ Jesus."* Vision IS movement! Paul says that he presses on toward a goal. He mentions a prize as his reward. My friend, your prize awaits you. Why stop now?

God later spoke to Jeremiah saying, *"For I know the thoughts that I think toward you, says the Lord, thoughts of peace and not of evil, to give you a future and a hope" (29:11).* God has a made-up mind about your future! For you, he has peace and hope! Begin now to move and see in the Spirit. Take your dreams captive. Tap into what God has in store for you. Knowing what God has in mind, who wants to sit still and relax? This leads us to the difference between personal ambition and God's vision for your life.

Vision vs. Ambition

It is important that you understand the difference between ambition and vision. Generally speaking, ambition is self-driven, while vision is God-driven. Note the differences:

Ambition	Vision
1. Ambitious people are filled with their own opinions and will.	1. Vision is all about the opinion of God and what His perfect will is for my life. *"Not my will but Your will, Lord, be done" (Matthew 26:39).*
2. Ambitious people believe in promoting themselves, their abilities; what they have done and are capable of accomplishing.	2. A true vision from God will always promote God, talk about what He has accomplished on the cross, and allow Him to sit on the throne, the position of authority.
3. Ambitious people will not easily give God glory. They take the glory for themselves.	3. A godly vision will give all the glory to God and to Him alone.
4. Ambitious people are fleshly motivated in order to build their own image.	4. Vision comes from being Holy Spirit-motivated. A vision that is Holy Spirit-driven will build the kingdom of God.

5. Ambitious people have their own desires and purposes high on their agenda.	5. A vision from God is all about His plans and purposes.
6. Ambitious people love to be in control in order to dominate or manipulate.	6. Anyone who has a true vision from God will have a servant's heart. A servant always makes room for others.
7. Ambitious people have a fire that is out of control. The fire will not purify, but destroy whoever gets in its way.	7. Vision is a fire under control, which brings Holy Spirit direction.
8. Ambitious people have one thing in mind. They **must** win. Ambitious people do not easily come under authority. They use other people as stepping stones in order to promote themselves.	8. Vision helps others win. A person with vision takes thousands with him or her and helps them all to be partakers of the blessings.

Obviously, people of vision stand in sharp contrast to ambitious people. As you can see, people of vision differ point by point with those who are motivated solely by ambition. Why not take additional time to compare ambition with vision, and see which force is at work in your life?

Jesus had a vision, and millions down through the centuries have benefited from it. He was not motivated by ambition while hanging on the cross; He was compelled to die because of His love for us. As a result, millions have become winners. Why? Jesus thought about others rather than Himself. His vision for lost mankind superceded His personal agenda. Remember, God's plan of redemption was fashioned in eternity past, long before the worlds began.

In the end, the visionary will be remembered over the ambitious person. How can you forget someone who helped you become a winner? The ambitious person will soon be forgotten because people grow weary of being used as a rung on someone else's ladder of success. In fact, an ambitious person generally becomes quite unpopular and overwhelmed with loneliness.

Matthew 6:22 says, *"If your eye is pure there will be sunshine in your soul" (TLB).* Vision will bring sunshine to your home, family, finances and many other segments of life. A pure eye is needed in order to clearly see the will of God. Leaders with "pure eyes" to see into the future will walk people into the sunshine of God's goodness and providence.

It is the revealed will of God that we live and enjoy a bright future. His revelations are like new rain that falls upon the earth. Without seeing the future, we are consigned to drought and even death. Vision will take us out, lift us up, and thrust us into something much bigger than we can imagine. Open your eyes and see Jesus! If you don't, you may focus your eyes on others, and that's not good.

What Isaiah Saw

Isaiah 6:1-3 says, *"In the year that King Uzziah died, I saw the Lord sitting on a throne, high and lifted up, and the train of His robe filled the temple. Above it stood seraphim; each one had six wings: with two he covered his face, and with two he covered his feet, and with two he flew. And one cried to another and said: Holy, holy, holy is the Lord of hosts: The whole earth is full of His glory."*

Isaiah saw what can only be seen in the Spirit realm. He saw the Lord through the eyes of the Spirit. What was his reaction? "WOE IS ME!" The prophet had a dramatic life-changing encounter with the Lord.

Any vision will first change the person to whom it was given.

It is difficult to listen to someone expound on a truth that has not changed his own life. That's why we need messages from the throne today, not just sermons. Sermons may be homiletically-sound and good; however, only messages that first change the preacher, change the people.

Look at chapter 5. The word *"woe"* is repeated six times in renouncing the sins of the people. Verse 11 says, *"Woe to those who rise early in the morning, that they may follow intoxicating drink; who continue until night, till wine inflames them!"*

Verse 18 says, *"Woe to those who draw iniquity with cords of vanity, And sin as if with a cart rope."*

Verse 20 says, *"Woe to those who call evil good, and good evil who put darkness for light, and light for darkness."*

Verse 21 says, *"Woe to those who are wise in their own eyes, And prudent in their own sight."*

Verse 22 says, *"Woe to men mighty at drinking wine. Woe to men valiant for mixing intoxicating drink."*

However, Isaiah's focus changes in chapter 6, as he is confronted with his personal sins. We tend to note rather easily the weaknesses of others, that is, until God turns our focus inwardly. Isaiah was changed by his own vision. The first purpose of a vision is to change the person who receives it.

If your vision is powerless to change you, how can you expect it to change the world?

Before we can expound the Word of the Lord that changes others, we first must be changed from *"glory unto glory."* Isaiah saw the Lord, and cried out, *"Woe is me."* Notice how the text shifts from "others" to "I." *"Behold, woe is me, for I am undone; because I am a man of unclean lips..." (verse 5).*

The presence of God, first and foremost, exposes our own shortcomings and sins. Surely, Isaiah lived close to God, for the prophet "saw the Lord!" That kind of intense relationship allowed him to see amazing things in the Spirit. Whoever sees in the Spirit will be changed. That person just cannot remain the same!

Isaiah's previous "woes" pointed outwardly to others; but the moment he saw the Lord, he began to look within. He saw the ugliness of his own flesh. Constantly looking at others' faults indicates a personal sin issue and reveals a problem in our relationship with God.

People who see in the Spirit are marked by genuine humility and brokenness.

When people come around them, they immediately sense the presence of Jesus, and feel welcome and free in their midst.

Have you ever been around someone who made you feel unholy? Their presence imposed a judgmental attitude and a man-made conviction upon you. Religious people always do that. But people who have seen the Lord, who have been changed in His presence, spread the aroma of Christ. Those around them are drawn by the awareness of His presence.

Isaiah 6:6-9 illustrates the beauty of a changed life and Isaiah's subsequent assignment from the Throne: *"Then one of the seraphim flew to me, having in his hand a live coal, which he had taken with the tongs from the altar. And he touched my mouth with it, and said; 'Behold, this has touched your lips; Your iniquity is taken away, And your sin is purged.' Also I heard the voice of the Lord, saying; 'Whom shall I send, And who will go for us?' Then I said, 'Here am I! Send me.' And He said, 'Go and tell this people: Keep on hearing, but do not understand; Keep on seeing but do not perceive.'"*

In verse 5 Isaiah confesses that he is a man of unclean lips. Significantly, when either Jeremiah or Isaiah had encounters with God, the first things to surfaced were their own weaknesses and sins. These men were not ashamed to admit their weaknesses. Both were transparent men. Sadly, we live in a world where people are hesitant to reveal their weaknesses. They choose to live in darkness. However, once we have entered into the presence of God, we have to deal with those "dark areas" in our lives in order to be effective in our Christian walk.

Again, any vision that does not change the receiver will never change others. God-given visions carry both the power of conviction and the power of deliverance. Isaiah was immediately convicted of sin in his life, confessed it, and was set free. We too, are like Isaiah. We easily identify the "woes" in other peoples' lives, but the moment we see in the Spirit we forget about others and begin to focus inwardly. True compassion comes into focus.

Isaiah was confronted with the holiness of God and his apparent need to die to sin and self. Interestingly, the chapter begins with these words, *"In the year that King Uzziah died, I saw the Lord..."* Uzziah's death in approximately 680 B.C. paralleled with Isaiah's encounter with God. Beyond chronological reasons, the passage also infers something specific about the nature of Uzziah, also known in Scripture as Azariah. The beginning of his reign was characterized by successful expeditions against the Edomites, the Philistines and Judah's other enemies. Uzziah also strengthened the walls of Jerusalem, and was a great patron of agriculture.

However, his end was less prosperous than his beginning. Elated with his splendid career, which spanned 52 years, he determined to burn incense on the altar of God, but was opposed by the high priests. The king became outraged at their resistance, and as he pressed forward with his censer, he was suddenly smitten with leprosy. Uzziah was determined to do it HIS way.

Someone aptly rendered this verse, "In the year that *'I'* died, I saw the Lord..." We must step down and surrender the throne of our lives to Christ. Self-centeredness and personal ambition reap only tragic results. For Uzziah, it was leprosy. God wants us to see as He sees. He wants us to move into the realm of the supernatural. But the only way we're going to reach our full potential and end well, is if we die to self. We must surrender our self-serving agendas to the Lord.

We live in a world of sickness, demonic bondage and evil spirits, which control our cities and countries. The time has come for us to die to sin and self, and take back what the enemy has stolen from us. Only then will we learn to move and see in the Spirit.

During this same encounter, God sent an angel with a coal of fire from off the altar and touched Isaiah's lips. The angel then announced that the prophet's sins were purged. We, too, desperately need a touch from God. It's the touch in the vision that gives it the ability to touch others, and even to touch the nations. You can only give what you have first received.

It's the "touch" in the vision that causes the vision to succeed.

Isaiah then heard a voice saying, *"Whom shall I send, and who will go for Us"* (verse 8)? God does not allow us to see in the Spirit or to receive visions just to advertise our spirituality. Any God-given vision carries responsibility. Isaiah says, *"I heard the voice of the Lord" (verse 8).* We must learn to discern the voice of the Lord! In today's world we are inundated with many voices. Sometimes it's difficult to tell the difference between God's voice and man's voice. Do you remember when Samuel, as a little boy, could not differentiate between the voice of God and the voice of Eli?

God asked Isaiah, *"Whom shall I send and who will go for Us?"* Perhaps you've been on a missions trip. Unfortunately, some missions trips become ego trips! People become the main attraction and God is robbed of the glory He deserves. Did you notice that the word "Us" is capitalized in verse 8? This plural pronoun refers to God the Father, Jesus the Son and the Holy Spirit.

When God sends us, we team up with the Godhead. It is an "Us" thing, not an "I" thing. What we do for the kingdom of God, we do with Him. He fulfills His purpose and goals through us. And He shares His glory with no one!

How do we learn to hear the voice of God? Through continued encounters with Him! Place my wife in a room filled with women who are talking, and I can readily identify her voice. How? I've been married to her for nearly 27 years, and I know her voice. Jesus said, *"My sheep hear my voice, and I know them, and they follow me" (John 10:27).* When you talk to someone enough times, his voice becomes easily identifiable. Isaiah said, *"I heard the voice of the Lord saying, "'Whom shall I send?'"* Isaiah had heard that same voice many times. He knew WHO was talking.

This question posed to Isaiah revealed God's motivation. God wants to SEND YOU OUT into the world. But first, you must be schooled in the things of the Spirit. You must be thoroughly trained and equipped. To successfully engage in spiritual warfare, you must know your enemy's strategies, and know how to use the weapons of the Spirit.

Remember, our *"weapons are not carnal, but mighty through God to the pulling down of strongholds" (2 Corinthians 10:4).* God's agenda is first and foremost. He will not give you a vision or a glimpse into the spirit world to exalt your name. He alone must receive the glory. Just think-- God chooses to use us to bring glory to His name. Aren't we blessed?

God's asked the prophet a second question, *"Who will go for Us?"* It is not a "you go" thing, or an "I go" thing. It is a "God go" thing. In His wisdom and sovereignty, God chose to expand His kingdom by using you and me. He does not expect you to go alone. He loves teamwork! The pronoun "Us" refers to teamwork.

When the time came for Jesus to enter Jerusalem, He asked His disciples to bring Him a donkey. Why a donkey? Why not a horse? The donkey did not know how to steal the glory of God! God never moves apart from His glory. His glory is part of him. By using a donkey, His glory was secure, as the donkey was not aware that it was to carry the Son of God. Had the donkey been aware of its heavenly rider, it could have stolen His glory. Sometimes God uses what we reject to insure that He receives all the glory.

After receiving a divine touch, Isaiah was instructed to *"Go and tell this people" (verse 9).* The strength and ability to go comes only from the touch of God upon our lives. Without His touch, we dare not go.

His touch commissions us.

Without it we become like gongs. A gong is the empty sound produced by someone who tries to accomplish something for God in his own strength. He makes a loud noise, but nobody listens! Nobody notices. Comparatively speaking, it would be like taking a teaspoon of water from out of the ocean. We impact other's lives only by the Spirit.

At the end of verse 8 we read these amazing words: *"Here am I! Send me."* These words came from the same man who previously cried out, *"I am undone. I am a man of unclean lips."* Initially, all of us come into His presence, our lives wrecked by sin, with nothing to boast about. Our sinful, fleshly nature makes us unacceptable. We must be spiritually overhauled. We need His touch! Grace and mercy turn total mishaps into people who can shout with a loud voice, *"Send me!"*

Isaiah's God encounter changed him from a self-centered man into a powerful voice for God. We, who are totally unworthy of such mercy, become channels through which the supernatural cleansing power of God can flow. We represent a holy God on earth!

Isn't this an amazing chapter? What Isaiah saw totally changed his life. The Lord continued to speak to Isaiah in verse 9. *"Go and tell this people: Keep on hearing, but do not understand. Keep on seeing, but do not perceive" (verse 9).* What was the Lord saying? The touch of God deepens our relationship with God and changes our speech, hearing, and perception.

Any true encounter with God includes the *TOUCH*, the *GO*, and the *MESSAGE*.

You cannot separate the three. Touching and not sending is senseless. Going without a clear message is worthless.

"Go and tell my people." God loves to communicate. He loves to talk with His people. His Word is pure and clean, and the human vessel that carries His Word must meet God's qualifications. Not everyone has the right to speak to others just because he heard from God. He must go through the right channels. He must know that he has been touched and sent, and he must have a clear message from the Lord.

Some messages are given by people who were obviously not touched or sent. Their word brings no deliverance or healing. The Bible reminds us in *2 Corinthians 3:6, "...For the letter kills, but the Spirit gives life."*

Words that sound good, but only tickle the ears of people, are just empty words. Compare his words with a man who has just walked out of the throne room of God. The latter can say with heaven's authority, *"Go tell this people."*

The story is told of two men who were asked to recite the twenty-third Psalm. The first man stood erect and proud and began to quote, *"The Lord is my shepherd...."* The crowd was amazed at his rhetoric and articulation. The second man, stood in confidence, but with a humble countenance. As he began to recite this Psalm of David, tears flowed freely within the room. His voice would break from time to time, followed by a pause. After both men had completed their recitations, one observer said, "The first man knew the psalm; the second man knew the shepherd."

Hallmark experiences in God forever etch themselves in our minds. Perhaps you remember where and when you came to know the Lord. Or where you were when you received the baptism in the Holy Spirit. Guess what? Your experience left with you! Your encounter with God followed you into the streets, malls and places of business. It traveled on planes, trains and automobiles! It crossed the oceans to foreign countries, and even walked the rural areas of life. God's intention was that your encounter brings change to your family, friends, cities and eventually, the world. It flies into places that you cannot imagine possible.

A God-given vision soars on its own wings.

David prayed in Psalm 55:6 and 7, "*Oh, that I had the wings of a dove! I would fly away and be at rest. I would flee far away and stay in the desert.*" This psalm was written after David's own son, Absalom, betrayed him by attempting to usurp the throne. When oppressed by evil people, or when the troubles of life bring fear, anguish and overwhelming anxiety, we too, often look to find rest and relief by escaping from our present distress. David found his refuge in God. The Early Church, as recorded in Acts 2, experienced a great "lift off" on the wings of the Holy Spirit.

God initiated a plan, through Christ, to lift humanity from the pit of sin, and to soar safely in this life and into eternity. His plan was formed from the very *"foundations of the world" (Ephesians 1:4)*. God has always been ready to share that plan with those who desire to see in the Spirit. Get in the Spirit; it's a fresh way of living! When you learn to see in the Spirit, you will be moved with compassion to act on what God shows you.

Eyes of Compassion

Those who are called by God are lovers of the Church. They do not want to see the Church harmed or destroyed by thieves. Do you remember the parable of the Good Samaritan? Luke 10:30 says, "*A certain man went down from Jerusalem to Jericho, and fell among thieves, who stripped him of his clothing, wounded him, and departed, leaving him half dead.*"

This verse prophetically illustrates how the Church sometimes deals with hurting people. When certain people finish "ministering," things end up worse than before. It looks like a "break in," instead of a "breakthrough!"

The devil's intention is to rip the Church apart, strip her of everything, wound her, and leave her to die. Given the enemy's character, we should not be surprised at such hideous tactics.

You have heard it said many times – wounded people wound people. Wounded people are many times as compassionless as the devil. Those who should bring healing, inflict wounds instead.

Jesus continues with the story in verses 31-37. Both a priest and a Levite see the man lying motionless on the road, and continue on their way. How tragic! The wounded man is a type of the Church. The priest and the Levite represent those in authority. One would think they would stop and help the poor man. Both had the recognition and the authority to offer assistance to this victim. They carried titles that were respected by the community, but neither of them had hearts that cared.

Perhaps if these scoundrels were alive today, they'd boast of ordination certificates that in theory, qualified them to minister. You know -- those framed, gold-embossed certificates that adorn many office walls. The ones stamped and signed by denominational officials! What good are these things if we have no heart for the bloody and needy in the streets of life?

Both of these religious people chose to pass by on the other side. They refused to get involved. Unfortunately, we live in a day when many people fear involvement. The Bible says they both *"looked and saw."* They merely glimpsed at the man. Just looking, without touching, will not heal burdens.

Simply looking will not help bleeding souls. Getting close to so-called clergy will not help you. We need more than titles and spectators. We need people with compassion to see the way God sees. NEEDED: people to get involved in the lives of wounded people.

Where would you and I be today had Jesus refused to get involved with the human race? What if He changed His mind two-thousand years ago and aborted God's plan of salvation? We would still be bound in sin! After all, Jesus had another option.

He could have summoned legions of angels to free Him from the cross. But thank God, the night before, while agonizing in the Garden of Gethsemane, He came to a resolve that changed the course of redemptive history. He prayed, *"Not my will but thy will be done" (Luke 22:42).* And the next afternoon He revealed the heart of the Father while hanging on that cruel Roman cross.

We were ripped apart by the devil and stripped of our dignity, but Jesus got involved. Thank God! When we were bloody and dying, He carried us to the inn of His mercy and grace. Driven by compassion, He looked down through the centuries, saw our dilemma, and gave of Himself. Today the human race has a room reserved at the inn of His grace. Have you secured your reservation? Call upon Him in faith today, lay your sins at His feet, and be made whole!

The man lay nearly dead in the street, and those who were equipped to help him, turned their heads the other way. What a heartbreaking story!

My friend, the OTHER SIDE is not an option for the believer. Without compassion, you will miss your destiny in Christ.

The parable of the Good Samaritan is a heart-rending account; however, there's a story behind the story. Deep racial tension existed between the Jews and the Samaritans. Seldom, if ever, did they interact; and for the most part, they hated one another.

In this parable, the assistance came from a despised Samaritan. Herein, lays one of life's great tragedies. Prejudice becomes an obstacle to meeting the needs of broken, wounded people. Many people are not even aware that prejudice exists in their lives.

The compassion demonstrated by the Samaritan becomes even more commendable when you think that, under normal conditions, he would not have even spoken to the man, much less nursed his wounds. Jesus came to bridge such divisions.

The Samaritan is a type of Jesus or the Holy Spirit. Mankind was lost in sin and destined for hell, but Jesus, Who was not welcomed on earth, came anyway. Four-hundred years had passed between Malachi and the time Jesus was born in Bethlehem. Communication between heaven and earth was silenced.

Prior to that, the entire human race had been plummeted into sin when Adam and Eve fell by way of transgression. But thank God for a Samaritan! Jesus did not think more of Himself, like the priest and the Levite, who chose to pass the other way. He thought of us! The Bible says, "He emptied Himself" and willingly left the splendors of heaven to come our way.

The Apostle Paul writes in Philippians 2:6-8, *"Who, being in the form of God, did not consider it robbery to be equal with God, but made Himself of no reputation, taking the form of a bondservant, and coming in the likeness of men. And being found in appearance as a man, He humbled Himself and became obedient to the point of death, even the death of the cross."*

Jesus could have stayed in heaven. He could have chosen to go another way, but out of His grace and mercy, He chose the way of the cross. He chose the way of compassion. He became a rejected, despised "Samaritan," whose blood alone qualified to save the world from sin. The Bible says in Luke 10:33 *"that when he saw the man, he had compassion."* He was compassion personified. You cannot buy or borrow compassion! A title will not make you compassionate. It is a work of the Spirit.

Compassion is an inner flow that pours out to the needs of others. Compassion loves to see people restored. Compassion reaches out; it never walks "by the other side." Ambition will walk by and not stop, but compassion always gets involved.

Vision mixed with compassion reaches out to hurting people; whereas, ambition focuses only on personal needs.

Do you remember the question God posed to Jeremiah? *"What do you see?"* The priest looked and saw the other side. The Levite looked and saw nothing. The Samaritan looked, and got involved. He, who had no authority in the religious order of his day, he who was rejected, revealed the heart of God.

Today, God is raising up men and women out of rejection, and using them to take the world by surprise. They will rescue the wounded Church from off the streets!

Certainly, our titles, ordination papers and wonderful scholastic abilities represent hard work and great potential. But if we have only ambition and no compassion, bloody people will continue to lie on the roads. The sight of their blood will not affect us, and they will receive no help. We must not glorify titles and minimize compassion. God sees potential in things that turn our heads. The priest and the Levite had titles, but not concern.

"But a certain Samaritan as he journeyed, came where he was. And when he saw him, he had compassion" (verse 33). Compassion is the driving force that compels us to minister to the hurting and wounded people around us. It drives us toward ministry.

To See Is To Do

Compassion is not compassion until acted upon. Thirst cannot be quenched without water. Wounds cannot be healed without medicine. To dream about compassion, makes it only a dream. When you think about compassion, it remains only a thought. When you talk about compassion, you engage in conversation only. But when you demonstrate compassion, it brings help and healing to others.

True compassion acts, while others idly stand by and ponder their level of involvement.

Luke 10:34 and 35 says, *"So he went to him and bandaged his wounds, pouring on oil and wine; and he set him on his own animal, brought him to an inn, and took care of him. On the next day, when he departed, he took out two denarri, gave them to the innkeeper and said to him, "Take care of him; and whatever more you spend, when I come again, I will repay you."* This was the heart of the Samaritan. It is also the heart of God. Sometimes His heart of compassion is demonstrated in places we least expect. At times, the heart of the Father cannot be found in the religious circles of the day. In this parable, the heart of the Father was found outside the circle of acceptance, among a people rejected by society at large.

The Samaritan wrapped him in bandages. He used his own oil and wine to attend the man's wounds. He did not charge him for services rendered. The time has come for us, as well, to give of ourselves, without expecting anything in return. The Samaritan assisted the wounded man, without thoughts of repayment.

We too, must get dying men and women off the road side of life and get them healed! The Samaritan put the man on his animal and took him to an inn. Notice that he did not say, "*If you'll tell me where your beast of burden is, I'll go get it, for mine is not available for you to use.*"

We are asked by God to use what we have to extend the Father's heart to people He brings our way. The inn doubled as a hospital. The Samaritan did not inquire about his medical plan or request his insurance card. His instructions to the innkeeper were clear: "*Take care of him, and whatever you spend, when I come back, I will repay you" (verse 35).*

This man unconditionally opened up both his heart and his wallet. Ambition refuses such generosity. Self-appointed leaders, who aspire toward personal greatness, make no such offers. Only people who have the heart of Christ emulate the Samaritan's heart of love. Essentially, the Samaritan said, "My bandages, oil, wine, transportation and finances belong to you." When compassion truly rules, it governs everything in your life!

At the conclusion of this parable, Jesus asked a question that demanded a verdict. Verse 36 says, "*So which of these three do you think was neighbor to him who fell among the thieves?*" Immediately, we learn how God defines success, and we are both surprised and challenged. The priest and Levite failed miserably, despite their prestigious titles. Again, the least and the rejected came forward to reveal the heart of God. In verse 37, we read the Lord's final instructions: *"Go and do likewise."*

What a challenge! To see is to do. The one who saw correctly was the one who did something. You need to see right, in order to do right. The ability to see right will help you to walk right. When we see the way God does, we don't have to ask, "Should I get involved?" This goes with seeing -- and goes without saying!

The priest and the Levite were prime examples of how Isaiah described the people of Judah. We read in 6:9, *"And he said, Go and tell this people, Hear ye indeed, but understand not; and see ye indeed, but perceive not."* The people were hearing, but not understanding. They were seeing, but not taking notice.

How many times did my parents ask me to take note of certain things when I was a teenager? Many times I did not assume responsibility when requested, especially if whatever it was did not concern me. I surely must have frustrated my parents.

We can travel through life seeing, yet not perceiving. We can walk, but not go anywhere. Talk, but not communicate. Know what we should do, but never take the initiative.

May God help us to not only see, but to perceive! We must not frustrate the grace of God. "Lord, open our eyes, and let us see You! Amen."

Paul Saw the Lord

The man's name is synonymous with leadership. We cannot mention him without talking about his accomplishments. He devoted much of his life plundering hell and populating heaven! He was Paul, the apostle, statesman, missionary, church planter, pastor, preacher, writer, and visionary. He devoted his life to taking the gospel to Gentile nations, and along the way, he wrote two-thirds of the New Testament. The beginning of his "true" ministry is recorded in Acts 9.

Saul of Tarsus, a zealous church leader from the tribe of Benjamin, exchanged his religion for a personal relationship with Jesus Christ. His name subsequently changed to coincide with his heart change. Saul became Paul. Paul, however, had quite a reputation before Acts 9. Although he had been actively involved in church work, he unfortunately, operated in what we previously termed "ambition." His ambition drove him to become what one man described as "the hatchet man of the Jews."

After his encounter with the risen Savior on the Road to Damascus, his life's motivation changed from ambition to vision.

What do we learn from Paul's wonderful testimony? We need our eyes opened before we can see the things of the Spirit.

We need an encounter with God in order to understand the spiritual world.

Acts 9 records the pivotal event in the life of this

great man. Countless others down through the centuries have experienced their own "Damascus Road" encounters with the resurrected Lord. Allow the Holy Spirit to give you insight into the life and ministry of this man. As you learn of God's unique dealings in Paul's life, respect and adoration will rise in your spirit. Like Paul, you too, can be changed. Just as God opened the eyes of this hit man-turned preacher, He can also open your spiritual eyes. Paul's conversion was powerful, his story unique; and God wants to touch and change you just like he did Saul of Tarsus.

Read Acts 9:1. *"Then Saul, still breathing threats and murder against the disciples of the Lord, went to the high priest and asked letters from him to the synagogues of Damascus, so that if he found any who were of the Way whether men or women, he might bring them bound to Jerusalem."* Note his untiring ambition. In his twisted attempts to work for God, he actually worked against God. Something was wrong in his thinking. He was spiritually blind.

Even today some Christians, who think they are working for the Lord are, in actuality, opposing the Work of God. They are led by ambition, not by spiritual sight.

Remember, ambition can be deceiving, especially if it causes people to oppose the things of God under the disguise of good works. Unfortunately, many times ambition is driven by a spirit of pride. Ambition exalts self and seldom makes room for others. "I" sits on the throne of ambition.

Ambitious people many times hurt others without caring. They bring harm to the body of Christ in order to reach their own goals. Typically, people who are motivated by fleshly-driven ambition become threatened by gifted individuals and those who possess strong leadership abilities. Many times, a spirit of control and domination rises to counteract these perceived threats.

As a result, ambition-centered people use others as stepping stones to accomplish what they think is good.

Saul of Tarsus, a religious zealot, thought he was doing God service by beating, imprisoning and even killing Christians!

People with vision, on the other hand, do not focus on themselves. Jesus demonstrated the difference between ambition and vision while hanging on the Cross. Putting His personal agenda aside, He chose to become the sacrificial lamb for the sins of lost mankind. Had ambition overridden vision, we would still be in our sins today, with no hope of eternal life.

Ironically, ambitious people harm the work of God. Saul of Tarsus actually believed that what he was doing was pleasing to God. His ambition became so intense and dangerous that God had to intervene. The very mention of his name struck terror in the lives of first-century Christians. The Bible indicates that he was an unofficial overseer at the stoning of their friend and deacon, Stephen. "*...And the witnesses laid down their clothes at a young man's feet, whose name was Saul" (Acts 7:58)*.

Afterwards, it took Barnabas some time to

convince the Jewish believers that Paul had changed. In truth, Paul's life really did not begin until after his Damascus Road encounter. Later he would testify that his life began at Calvary! His life changed from "I-centered" ambition to "Christ-centered" vision. Ambition was the motivating force that drove him, that is, until Jesus arrested him "on the way."

Had Jesus thought only of Himself on the cross, the plan of salvation would have been aborted. But Jesus was willing to lay down His life for the vision that consumed Him. God-given vision makes room for others. A familiar chorus says, "He was nailed to the cross for me." Vision overrode personal ambition, and God's plan of salvation remained intact.

If we are not willing to hurt, much less die for our vision, we probably have not received a vision from God.

People today will follow leaders who are saturated with vision. Leaders, if need be, are willing to die for what they believe. Anything not worth dying for is not worth living for. Billy Graham's late father-in-law, L. Nelson Bell, said, "Only those who are prepared to die are really prepared to live."

We can now live forever because Jesus died to give us eternal life. If the Son of God loved you so much that He was willing to die for you, then the least you can do is live for Him! A true revelation of Jesus brings this kind of resolve. We need to see in the Spirit.

According to Acts 9:2, it was Paul's intention to

bring the people of the Way bound to Jerusalem. What he didn't understand at the time was that free people cannot be bound! Ropes and chains may bind hands and feet, but they cannot bind the spirit of a man or woman.

What was wrong with Saul of Tarsus? He knew the Scriptures. Being a highly intellectual man, he was well-versed in the law. How could he make such colossal mistakes? How could he be so blind? The answer is simple. Like others who are spiritually blind, Paul was deceived by an "18-inch error." He possessed much intellect, but had no heart knowledge.

The distance from your head to your heart determines the difference. You can know the Bible well, and still not have a changed heart. That's why Paul could speak with authority when he would later write to Timothy concerning men in the last days, *"Ever learning, and never able to come to the knowledge of the truth" (2 Timothy 3:7).* Paul too, originally had knowledge apart from an experience with God.

As a Pharisee, Paul's authority came from the letters he carried from the high priest. He understood the letter of the law. He had the logos but not the *rhema.* His mind was well developed; however, he knew nothing of the Spirit world. Later, His authority would come from the Spirit! Paul's spiritual eyes had been opened. Only godly intervention could bring that kind of change.

Acts 6:3-6a describes the birth of a dynamic ministry. "*And as he journeyed, he came near Damascus: and suddenly there shined round about him a light from heaven: And he fell to the earth, and heard a voice saying unto him, 'Saul, Saul, why are you persecuting me?' And he said, Who are you Lord? And the Lord said, "I am Jesus whom you are persecuting…"*

Your wall may be covered with theological certificates of achievement. You may know the Bible thoroughly from Genesis to Revelation. You may be a Greek and Hebrew scholar. But do you know Jesus? Knowledge can be your enemy if you never allow Him to change your heart. God is Spirit, and you will only know Him if you know Him in the Spirit.

Technically speaking, you cannot study God. If this were true, then only intellectually-minded people would be able to know God. Remember, just gathering facts about someone does not mean that you know him. I know a lot of facts about famous people, but I can't say that I really know them. I know quite a bit about George W. Bush, but I don't personally know the man. Similarly, we can study about God as He is revealed in the Scriptures and still not know the God of the Scriptures personally. We are introduced to Him by the Spirit, Who in-dwells us.

Do you remember your courting days? You learned a lot of facts about your future mate. Perhaps you thought you knew him or her well. However, it wasn't until you actually lived with your spouse that you got to know the "real" person.

I can give you many facts about my wife's personality, but you still will not know her. I truly know her because we have lived together for 27 years.

Knowing about God is not the same as knowing God. Sadly enough, many who know about God, will miss heaven by 18 inches because they never really "knew" God. Relationship brings life. Religion deceives and brings spiritual death.

Again, the only way for you to know God is to know Him in the Spirit. *John 4:24 says, "God is Spirit, and those who worship Him must worship in spirit and in truth."*

You cannot study "spirit." You can only walk in the Spirit. You may ask, "How do I walk in the Spirit?" I'm glad you asked. I have good news for you!

Man was the crowning glory of God's creation. The Creator saved the best for last! We are different than the rest of God's creation. The life cycle of animals ends at death. Plants seasonally come and go. Even the big fishes in the seas have limited life spans. Why? Unlike humans, they do not possess spirits.

You and I live in a body, sense with our soul, and respond to God with our spirit. When our body dies, our soul and spirit live on. That's why we are called the crown of God's creation. Genesis 1:26 says, *"Let us make man in our own image, according to Our likeness; let them have dominion over the fish of the sea, over the birds of the air, and over the cattle, over all the earth and over every creeping thing that creeps on the earth."*

You were made in the image of the Triune God. When the devil looks at you, he remembers God. God now has His image on the earth. That's why the devil hates mankind so much, especially regenerated mankind. That's why he hates the womb. Every child "looks" like God. Satan's diabolical scheme of abortion represents his attempt to stamp out God's image on earth. Every fetus is a possible threat to his kingdom, and a reminder of Jesus Christ. This would not be the case if mankind possessed only a "body."

The devil hates the fact that we are body, soul and spirit. When we come to know Christ personally, we have potential to bring great damage to the devil's kingdom.

As the crowning glory of God's creation, we not only look like Him, but we have the ability to commune with Him. We can know Him intimately! God is Spirit, and *"in Him we live, we move and we have our being" (Acts 17:28).*

In summary, every human being, created in the image of God, receives a deposit of God's Spirit. He can meet and communicate with God in a wonderful and refreshing way when he walks in the Spirit.

To know Him by the Spirit requires that we bypass our mind mechanism. Although our mind plays a unique role in our walk with God, we must go a step further and walk in the Spirit.

We are told to have the mind of Christ; however, our spirit man must override our soul, if we are to walk in the Spirit. Our soul (intellect, will and emotions) must always subject itself to the Spirit of God.

A grand old hymn of the Church says, "…And He walks with me, and He talks with me, and He tells me I am His own…" Isn't it wonderful to know that we can communicate with God in the Spirit?

The Apostle Paul, of course, possessed knowledge. He had a very well-developed mind. He was a giant of reasoning. But in Acts 6:3 he came into contact with another world. The resurrected Savior spoke to him from out of heaven! He would never again be the same man. The Holy Spirit changed his life.

From then on, his life would be governed by the Spirit of God. He would no longer solely rely upon his intellect. Later, this great preacher to the Gentiles would testify, *"And my speech and my preaching were not with persuasive words of human wisdom, but in demonstration of the Spirit and of power" (1 Corinthians 2:4).* How could Paul make such a statement? What happened to him on the road to Damascus flowed out into his life and ministry.

You can never demonstrate what you don't have!

Paul's Acts 9 experience later put him on the evangelistic circuit. That crisis experience changed the course of his life. He was now connected to heaven. Never again would he operate in the same way. From that time on, the operative word in his life would be "change." Only the Holy Spirit can accomplish that!

Eyes Suddenly Opened!

Suddenly. I love this word! It describes the modus operandi of the Holy Spirit. The sudden experiences of God come exactly as the Word indicates – without warning. When the angelic host announced the birth of Jesus to unsuspecting shepherds, *"suddenly a light shone from heaven" (Luke 2:9).*

In order to remove darkness from the life of Paul, God blinded him with light. To remove any darkness from our lives, we need light!

The light of God deals with the darkness of fleshly ambition. Someone as spiritually hardened as Saul needed to be dealt with in a sudden way. God did not deal with him on the basis of reasoning. He dealt with him decisively and suddenly. Saul received no warning!

No one can ever prepare for the "suddenlies" of God, or even know when to expect such a move. Sometimes God moves suddenly in His Church. His strategy does not allow us time to reason, as there is always someone ready to analyze the ways of God.

In Acts 9:4, something happens to Paul, that I'm sure, pressed him beyond his religious comfort zone. He fell to the ground! God and Saul of Tarsus met in the dust.

People who experience dramatic encounters with God really don't care about environment. Both the need and desire to be changed and to have their eyes opened override any exterior factors. Believe me, Paul was not the type who would easily fall. No courtesy falls for this Jew of Jews!

Another "dusty" encounter took place between

the pre-incarnate Christ and Jacob, as recorded in Genesis 32:22-32. Jacob, who was about to meet up with his brother Esau after many years, had sent his two wives, concubines and eleven sons on ahead. This left him alone in the camp, and a *"man came and wrestled with him until dawn" (NLT).*

Like Paul, Jacob could not win his match against heaven. In his battle with God he, too, raised dust; and after the dust settled, he came out limping because his hip socket had been knocked out of joint. When God deals decisively with us, and the "dust" settles, we too walk (or limp) away having our flesh conquered. Our fleshly resistance dies in the dirt!

During the sudden visitations of God, time does not allow us to analyze whether or not it happens "decently and in order." The man from Tarsus was, in a split second, hit by a blinding light, knocked to the ground, and heard a voice. His life was transformed! He had an encounter of the God kind.

Isaiah experienced a similar, but not-so-dramatic encounter centuries earlier. Both men, nonetheless, were changed! This Old Testament prophet also saw the Lord, and, in all probability, fell to the ground, reeling under the weight of his sin. We too, hear the voice of God during those dramatic heavenly encounters in our lives.

Acts 9:1 records how Saul persecuted the people of the Way. In verse 4 the Lord pointedly asks him, *"Saul, Saul, why are you persecuting me?"* Remember, what you do against anyone who belongs to Christ, you do against God! God opposed Saul's ministry style in verse one, and subsequently took measures to show this "Pharisee of the Pharisees" that he was working against heaven itself. He got Saul's attention!

In verse 5 we learn just how little Saul knew about the Spirit of God. His ignorance is unintentionally revealed when he asks, *"Who are you, Lord?"*

Here was a man who possessed much knowledge about the law and the prophets. He had thoroughly studied the Pentateuch, but did not know the Author! Although Saul previously exhibited much confidence in his knowledge of facts, he still had to ask the Lord to identify Himself. Saul, who in the process of becoming Paul, demonstrated the truth that you cannot know God simply on the basis of facts. To know Him, you must move in the Spirit.

"Who are you Lord" (verse 5)? Really, he answered his own question when he said, "Lord." When we have an encounter with the God of heaven, we do not have to second guess as to His identity. Nor do we have to ask others, "Who was that?" Anyone who has a genuine encounter with God knows it!

Paul lay amazed and trembling on the ground. *"Lord, what will you have me to do" (verse 6)?* Paul knew to whom he was speaking. As we spend more time in the presence of God, we too, find answers for the dilemmas that come into our lives. We learn to rely less on what others think. Answers to unsolved matters and difficult issues come easier when we learn to hear His voice.

In verse 5 the clear revelation and answer came as the Son of God spoke from heaven: *"I am Jesus whom you are persecuting."* Paul is made to realize that, in reality, the Church was persecuting itself.

Sometimes what we label as the work of the Lord, God calls persecution. That's why we must hear directly from the Lord. We cannot know for sure if we are doing the right thing, or following God's path, unless we've had a direct encounter with God Himself.

How many times have we worked for the Lord, not realizing that we were really working against the Lord? How many times have we hidden behind the work of the Lord to fight our brothers and sisters? How many times have we used the name of Jesus to justify our impure motives? Or to get what we want? Remember, we all carry the image of God. When we walk blindly, not obeying the voice of the Spirit, we work against the Lord. Jesus confronted Paul with this very issue. He worked against God's plan and purpose and Jesus said to him, *"You are persecuting me" (verse 4).*

This brings tremendous shame on the Church. It also brings confusion. Imagine how excited the enemy gets when believers fight one another. They, sadly enough, aid and abet the enemy during those times. He then takes the opportunity to re-group his camp. The eyes of our spirit must be open to suppress the enemy's tactics.

After the Lord got Paul's attention and understanding, Paul asks, *"What do you want me to do" (verse 6)?* This is an extraordinary turn of events, as Paul was usually the one barking out threats and orders. He was a teacher and a commander. He operated using brute force. However, when confronted by Jesus, he asked the questions and Jesus gave the instructions!

Without the anointing upon our lives, we accomplish nothing of eternal significance.

We function helplessly when we rely upon fleshly ideas. God told Paul, *"Go into the city and you will be told what to do" (verse 6).* The one, who was used to giving instructions, immediately obeyed the heavenly vision. Paul came under new ownership that day! Surely, God knows how to humble us!

In verse 8 we return to the theme of this book. *"What do you see?"* The heavenly light had blinded Paul. God had to blind him physically, so he could discover his spiritual eyes.

Sometimes we need to temporarily lose something important in order to gain an appreciation for what really matters.

We need to be removed from our comfort zone. Paul's real ministry was mapped out before him, although at the time he had no idea what God had planned for him. His ministry itinerary would include *"much suffering."*

Likewise, you have a ministry inside that needs to come forth, but will only be discovered as you submit to the presence of God. Natural abilities are not the strength of any ministry. God wants you to walk humbly before Him, and allow Him to unleash your kingdom potential. Don't resist like Paul, and have to be knocked down!

Afterwards, Paul's traveling companions led him into Damascus. In verse 1 Paul was in control of circumstances. By verse 4, he had lost control. Lose what you have. Get rid of what you're hanging on to. You may think it valuable, but it pales in comparison to being blind for three days! We, too, need times of doing without. It is during those times that we become spiritually sensitive to the voice of God, and we comparison to what God has in store for you.

Paul was blind for three days. We, too, need times of doing without. It is during those times that we become spiritually sensitive to the voice of God, and we more readily discover what God has waiting for us. Paul's life was set on a new course – one targeted for ministry. He lost control in order to receive God's true vision for his life, and subsequently gained new control.

Sometimes God has to strip us of everything in order for us to receive much.

Why did God blind his new servant? Paul had to get rid of the things he thought he needed in order to get the things he really needed. This man, whose reputation preceded him, and who knew the Scriptures, was informed, bold, equipped and religious. His credentials were impressive. However, he did not need a letter from the high priest; he needed an encounter with Almighty God!

Verse 9 says that Paul lost his appetite. *"...And (for three days) neither did eat nor drink."* Like Job, this new convert could say, *"I have esteemed the words of his mouth more than my necessary food" (23:12).*

When we become so consumed with the

presence of God, even the need to eat dissipates. Our hunger turns toward spiritual things. What previously seemed important becomes trivial. Saul turned Paul, was "Exhibit A."

The Spirit overrides the knowledge and wisdom of man and empowers him to change.

God is not against knowledge. He tells us that *"the fear of the Lord is the beginning of knowledge" (Proverbs 1:7).* Paul was off to a great start! Interestingly enough, God used Paul's extensive knowledge of the Scriptures, combined it with his ability to see in the Spirit, and eventually used him to write two-thirds of the New Testament! He's the God of wisdom!

Verse 10 introduces a man by the name of Ananias. The Bible simply refers to him as a disciple. This obscure believer had something Paul did not: well-developed eyes to see in the Spirit. Ananias was tuned in to the Holy Spirit!

God spoke to him in a vision and said, *"Arise and go to the street called Straight, and inquire at the house of Judas for one called Saul of Tarsus for behold he is praying" (verse 11).* God gave this wonderful servant an awesome vision. Note the following details:

1. God showed him the name of the street -- Straight.
2. God showed him the owner of the house -- Judas.
3. God showed him who he was looking for -- Saul.
4. God told him ahead of time where Paul

came from -- Tarsus.

5. And finally, God showed Ananias what Paul would be doing when he arrived -- Praying.

Isn't this amazing? Ananias was an ordinary disciple, a follower of Jesus, who saw and moved in the Spirit.

Ananias was obedient to the heavenly vision. The miracle continued, as God informed Paul of his coming, and commanded him to place his hands on Paul. And when he did, not only was Paul's physical eyesight restored, but his spiritual eyes were opened. A new world opened up before him!

We too, must change. Our eyes must be opened. We need to see things the way God see them. Paul would never be the same again. He experienced a total transformation. Later, he would write to the Church at Corinth, *"If any man be in Christ, he is a new creation: old things have passed away; behold all things have become new" (2 Corinthians 5:17).* His was indeed the voice of experience!

Paul had to reach a complete standstill in his life to discover his real calling. He exchanged one ministry for another – deception for truth. He went from hurting the Church to healing the Church. His goals, destiny and purpose for living were altered in the dust. He discovered that the "real" Paul was spiritually blind. Divine intention and intervention put him on the right track.

Our flesh needs to be neutralized completely before we can focus on the spirit man. Paul was blinded, so he could see! The driving force in his life, previous to his Damascus Road encounter, was ambition. That's why God had to temporarily take away his sight.

Hymn writer, John Newton, who penned these infamous words, "I once was blind, but now I see," certainly described the Apostle Paul. Paul's fleshly ambition now turned to an all-consuming vision and passion for God.

Incredibly, when God opened Paul's spiritual eyes, he saw certain things very clearly. He saw Ananias coming into the house on Straight Street and laying hands on him. He saw the scales fall off his eyes. Amazingly, the gift to see in the Spirit was there all the time; however, his personal ambitions had overridden his gift within.

Acts 9:13 and 14 says, *"Then Ananias answered, "Lord, I have heard from many about this man, how much harm he has done to your saints in Jerusalem. And he has authority from the chief priests to bind all who call on your name."*

How dangerous it is when we work for God with wrong motives! Paul stood in direct opposition to the plan of God for his life, while all the time thinking he was doing God a favor. The Early Church feared Paul more than they feared the devil.

Attacks that come from inside are unexpected and highly dangerous. Obviously, the devil constantly tries to ambush God's people, but we have weapons to combat his attacks. However, we have no defense against combatant brothers. It is most unfortunate and heartbreaking when brothers fight one another. The only remedy when this happens is to get into the presence of God, and to seek His vision for our lives.

Paul would never again be the same. His focus forever changed. He now played according to a new set of rules. He marched to the beat of a different drummer.

Natural humiliation brought spiritual exaltation.

A dead end brought a new beginning. Paul was ushered into the greatest years of his life. When changes come into someone's life we use the phrase, "They're playing a different ballgame." Paul was soon placed on hell's hit list because he had discovered a new world.

Some years ago, I was invited to minister in Malawi. While there I was invited to go swimming in a very large lake. Someone suggested that I swim under water and open my eyes. I did and what a surprise! I discovered a colorful world of fish and other wonders. It was a world of splendor and beauty, unspoiled by man. It was virtually untouched and at peace with nature. Who would have guessed that such an underwater pageantry existed?

Similarly, if we are willing to daily submit our lives to the Lord, we will make wonderful discoveries in the Spirit world. Our natural behavior cannot remain the same once we've been exposed to the Spirit.

The enemy hates it when you exchange your driving force of ambition for vision. When you begin to move in the Spirit, you become a major threat to the kingdom of darkness.

Hell lost a key player that day on the road. Saul of Tarsus became "public enemy number one" in the regions of darkness. He began to persecute his real enemy, instead of the Church. In addition, the religious establishment of the day rose up in anger. Those who accomplish great exploits for God always stir up religious authorities.

Finally, it must have been difficult for Ananias to deliver the last part of God's message to Paul. *"Go, for he is a chosen vessel of mine to bear my name before Gentiles, kings and the children of Israel. For I will show him many things he must suffer for my name's sake" (Acts 9:15 and 16).* And indeed he suffered.

The greater the ministry,
the greater the cost.
Anything that costs nothing,
accomplishes nothing.

Although Paul met with great resistance during the ensuing years, his ministry touched countless thousands of lives. Understand that the greater the resistance, the greater your ministry! Prior to his conversion, the Church suffered persecution because of Paul's ambition. During his post-conversion years this great visionary paid the price himself.

Today it seems that most everyone is talking about change. For most people, however, change does not come easily. To change, you must admit that you were wrong, or at least on a dead end street. It means that you are ready to take another route.

Paul's life was forever changed while on the road to Damascus. The remainder of his life was spent in the service of Christ. As you study his writings, and what others wrote about him, you cannot help but chart his growth and maturity as a believer. Saul of Tarsus became Paul the Apostle.

Acts 15:36-41 records a contentious meeting that took place between Paul and Barnabas over John Mark's credibility as a minister. Paul and Barnabas subsequently parted company. God used Paul's reaction, however, to expand the Early Church's missionary enterprise. Not one, but two missionary teams departed that day to spread the gospel. Barnabas and Mark, along with Paul and Silas, took to the roads to present Christ to their lost and dying generation.

The story, however, does not end with this tension-filled meeting. Years later, an older and more refined Paul would become a mentor to young preachers. Over time, the Holy Spirit would continue to chip away the rough edges in Paul's life. When writing to Timothy toward the end of his life, Paul would say, *"Only Luke is with me. Take (John) Mark. And bring him with you: for he is profitable to me for the ministry" (2 Timothy 4:11).* Conversion is the miracle of a moment; discipleship is a life-long process. At the end of his life, he was able to say, *"I have fought a good fight, I have finished my course, I have kept the faith" (2 Timothy 4:7).*

Throughout his ministry, Paul used his Damascus Road encounter as his only defense. Time and again, he recounted the story of his conversion. In Acts 22 he stood before an accusing, angry mob in Jerusalem and detailed his experience on the road. In Acts 26, he stood before King Agrippa, taking yet another opportunity to share his testimony. In Ephesians we find him under house arrest, chained to a soldier. Can you imagine being chained to the Apostle Paul, indisputably the Early Church's foremost soul winner?

It all began in Acts 9. A heart of stone was changed to a heart of flesh. As a matter of fact, fellow Christians were suspect because of his reputation. Many doubted the authenticity of his experience. However, his initial encounter with Christ brought both undeniable and immediate changes into his life.

How about you? Have you invited Jesus to come into your life? He wants to instantaneously change your life today. Just ask Him!

Encounters of the "Seeing" Kind

What took place after Paul's dramatic encounter with Jesus? *"Immediately he preached Christ" (Acts 9:20).* Note the operative word, "immediately," and the phrase "preached Christ." Immediately means "now."

A divinely-changed life must find ways to express its witness. Right now is the most acceptable time! Paul preached Christ. Nothing else mattered. His personal ambitions died that day in the dust. The predominant love of his life would be preaching. His theme was *"Christ and Him crucified" (I Corinthians 1:23).* Jesus, plus nothing else, had dramatically changed his life. Jesus was his message!

Upon hearing of his conversion to Christianity, the Jews plotted to kill Saul. This one, who had killed others, now had a bounty on his head. Saul turned Paul, was responsible for killing or imprisoning believers in the past. Now his life was in danger.

The moment you have an encounter with God, and begin to make a significant difference, you will be hated by others. A man with a vision will not be accepted in all circles.

Jesus, the Son of God, brought a vision to earth, but He was not accepted. He was rejected and ultimately crucified. However, because of what He accomplished on the cross -- the fulfillment of the Father's vision – His influence lives on. He came to redeem the human race, and He triumphed! The same Jesus Who so dramatically impacted Saul of Tarsus, still changes lives today.

When a visionary dies, his works live on.

When ambitious people die, their works die with them. Typically, those with ambition cause harm to people, and nobody wants to remember them. Does the name Adolph Hitler sound familiar?

His personal ambition to develop a "superior race" resulted in the deaths of six-million people. After more than 60 years, people are still trying to erase the memory of this mad man. His life illustrates the power of ungodly ambition.

But our Savior left heaven with a vision to redeem a lost race. His atoning death on the cross took away our sins and sicknesses. The divine exchanges that took place that day encompassed His vision. He took our sins and gave us His righteousness. He bore our sicknesses and gave us healing. Millions can testify to His life-changing power. He will be remembered and worshiped forever and ever. Give Him praise!

Had Paul not encountered Christ on the road to Damascus, he would have been remembered as a murderer. But by the grace of God, Paul the Apostle is remembered as the preacher to the Gentiles. He gave his life for the Gospel. To this day, multitudes are influenced by the vision he had to expand the kingdom of God. Much has been written about Paul. History reveals that he became a great church leader.

In fact, the focus in the book of Acts changes from Peter to Paul in chapter 9. Both were entrusted leaders of the Early Church. This leads us to partially examine the subject of leadership.

To See or Not to See: Three Types of Leaders

You cannot mention the Apostle Paul without discussing his great leadership abilities. Time and again, in the book of Acts and throughout his epistles, Paul is seen as a leader of leaders. Not only did he found and pastor churches, he mentored young men in the Faith; and in his apostolic office, he gave oversight to groups of churches.

In Acts 15, he helped to arbitrate what became known as the Jerusalem Council. The issue in that council centered on the matter of circumcision. Must Gentiles be circumcised after coming to faith in the Lord Jesus?

"When therefore Paul and Barnabas had no small dissension and disputation with (the men from Judea), they determined that Paul and Barnabas, and certain others of them, should go up to Jerusalem unto the apostles and elders about this question" (Acts 15:2). Even though it was James, the pastor of the church in Jerusalem, who moderated the meeting, it was Paul who swayed the council toward its final conclusion. Peter waxed theologically eloquent in verses 7-11; but it was Paul who stood (verse 12) and confirmed that *"miracles and wonders were being wrought among the Gentiles by them (Paul and Barnabas)."* Paul reasoned that God's grace was being extended not only to the Jews, but to the Gentiles as well.

Peter also exerted much influence during this historic council. *"And when there had been much disputing, Peter rose up, and said unto them, Men and brethren, ye know how that a good while ago God made choice among us, that the Gentiles by my mouth should hear the word of the gospel, and believe. And God, which knoweth the hearts, bare them witness, giving them the Holy Ghost, even as he did unto us; And put no difference between us and them, purifying their hearts by faith. Now therefore why tempt ye God, to put a yoke upon the neck of the disciples, which neither our fathers nor we were able to bear" (verses 7-10)?*

Paul presented an argument based on personal ministry and Peter gave a theological treatise. James kept order!

Directed by the leadership abilities of Paul, Peter and James, the council reached a final decision. Verse 11 summarized their final position, *"But we believe that through the grace of the Lord Jesus Christ we shall be saved, even as they (Gentiles)."* Paul's aggressive leadership skills came into play several years later when he withstood Peter *"to the face in Antioch" (Galatians 2:11).*

Somehow, Peter had succumbed to the pressure of Judaizers, who were once again proclaiming that Gentiles must be circumcised to be truly saved. Peter's fear of public opinion caused him to back down on this all-important position. The Bible says that when Peter came to Antioch, Paul confronted him about his double-mindedness.

The leader within Paul surfaced. Peter was opposed and rebuked. Scriptures indicate that Peter recognized his error and accepted Paul's reproof in a humble and repentant manner. He later referred to Paul as *"our beloved brother Paul" (2 Peter 3:15).* Leadership is an awesome responsibility. Godly, Spirit-led leadership is non-negotiable. Leaders must see in the Spirit. Today we see three kinds of leaders in the Church -- self-appointed, man-appointed and God-appointed.

Self-appointed Leaders

These individuals push themselves to the forefront and always cause trouble. They are motivated by selfish ambition. They pretend to care, but their real desire is to build their own image and kingdom. Unfortunately, they always mislead a few. Their work leads to confusion and strife.

Self-appointed leaders are easily spotted because of their unwillingness to submit to authority. Their self-centered approach to ministry causes them to despise authority. Because they are self-serving, the authority at hand never appoints them. In retaliation, they appoint themselves. Obviously, these people cause conflict with the authority structures put in place by God. Understand that these self-appointed leaders usually accuse those in godly authority of being dictators. Eventually, their true colors are revealed, as what they judge in others becomes exposed in their own lives.

God appoints delegated authority in His Church. The Holy Spirit only anoints what He appoints!

Sadly, self-appointed leaders deceive undiscerned, unsuspecting believers. They many times capitalize on their personality gifts to draw away weak followers from God's righteous authority. They hate accountability, and refuse to accept checks and balances in their lives. Many self-appointed leaders deceivingly use the Lord's Name to justify their actions. "We are accountable only to God," they say.

However, the Bible illustrates time and again that God's finest leaders submitted themselves to one another. Many leaders who practice deception do it unknowingly, and unwittingly harm many people. This is hard to understand. Be careful!

Man-appointed Leaders

Man-appointed leaders, at some point in time, will let you down. They remain popular as long as they dance to the tune of those who elected them. Popular vote is not always God's vote. Do you remember the story of Joshua and Caleb found in Numbers 13? Moses sent out twelve men to spy out the Promised Land. The group returned to present their report. Ten of them gave an evil report, but Joshua and Caleb spoke through the eyes of faith. *"We can well-possess the land" (Numbers 13:30),* they said. The vote was 10-2 in favor of staying put. The majority won and the will of God was thwarted. Joshua and Caleb voted with their spiritual eyes. The other ten, who were self-appointed leaders, voted through eyes of unbelief.

Most of the time, man-appointed leaders are popular as long as they please the voters. When pressure comes, they crumble in fear. These leaders rely largely upon their abilities and talents; however, this very criteria many times leads to their downfall.

The tried and true elements of leadership are a true call from God and character. As long as man-made leaders impress people, they will continue to be appointed.

Real leaders, however, are called to impress God!

I would rather be God-appointed, with character as my foundation, than to submit my future to the whims of men. God always backs His appointments! His divine support system will never fail you.

God-appointed Leaders

God-appointed leaders always take people to a higher level in Christ. What God pours into them, they invest in others. Anything that comes from God challenges us and takes us higher. Neither self nor man has access to these leaders. These leaders get their instructions directly from God and no one else. While they remain open to wise counsel from godly sources, their ultimate direction comes from the throne-- unlike self-appointed and man-made leaders, who have no protection,

God-appointed leaders remain under "the shadow of His wings."

They choose not to rely on popularity or good circumstances. They see in the Spirit, and in due time, announce their directions to others. The end result is divine fruit and stability that benefits everyone under their influence.

God-appointed leaders possess a spirit of excellence. These leaders have first accepted challenges by God. God challenges can only be endured by God-appointed leaders. *Ezekiel 37:1 says, "...The hand of the Lord came upon me and brought me out in the Spirit of the Lord, and set me down in the midst of the valley; and it was full of bones. Then he caused me to pass by them all around, and behold, there were very many in the open valley; and indeed they were very dry. And He said to me, "Son of man, can these bones live?" So I answered, "O Lord God, You know."*

Ezekiel answered God's call to minister to a most unusual audience. His view of the valley coincided with an assignment. The prophet was called to minister in a dead, dry place.

God called me in 1971 to minister to the nations. Now, thirty-two years later, I am actively spreading the gospel around the world.

Get ready, God-appointed people! With your vision comes hard work. Visions are not for lazy people. When God gives you a vision, He shows you only the end result. He does not show you the in-between details.

The beneficiary of the God-appointed leader is God and His kingdom.

The secondary beneficiary is the leader himself, and all who follow him. Allow me to reiterate. Only those leaders appointed by God take us to higher levels. These wonderful leaders are usually appointed during times of sudden and intense visitation. Would you agree that Ezekiel's assignment in the valley was bone rattling?

God-appointed leaders thrive on challenge.

How can you tell when a leader rejects the challenges of God? He opposes change and becomes critical. Critics are birthed from the ranks of those who stubbornly refuse to move with God. Often, visionaries fall prey to the luxury of comfort zones, and subsequently refuse to change. To resist change is to stagnate. True God-appointed leaders refuse to wallow in the mud hole of criticism. They are partakers!

Remember, the only way you can do nothing wrong is to do nothing.

Those who aim at nothing hit it every time! I would rather do something, make mistakes, be criticized and accomplish something; than do nothing, make no mistakes, never be criticized, and have nothing to show for my life when I stand before God some day.

Generally speaking, along with three types of leaders in our churches, come three types of people. They are the undertakers, the caretakers and the risk takers.

Not Always 20/20: Three Types of People

What are some of the characteristics of undertakers, care-takers and risk takers? Let's look at these three types of people.

Undertakers

Undertakers are always negative. Everything they see is filtered through dark lenses. They always look for the bad, listen for what's wrong, and operate in doubt and unbelief.

If someone says the sky is blue, they say it's gray and dismal. Call something white, and they say it's black. They carry a spirit of death, and always expect the worse. They operate in fear. Negative people, if allowed, quickly influence those who draw near. Oppose their negative confession, and you become their enemy.

Unfortunately, I have witnessed many pastors over the years embrace the spirit of the undertaker. It is a killer!

Caretakers

Caretakers are neither negative, nor are they positive. They function in a neutral capacity. They certainly are not visionaries. While they typically do a good job, they become uncomfortable outside of routine. They are extremely predictable. They accept things as they are and never try to change them. They do not destroy anything, but neither will they improve anything. If you met a caretaker in 1953, and met him again in 2003, you would note that he had not changed one bit! He would be exactly the same person!

Caretakers need strong leaders who can take them to higher ground. The word "potential" is not in their dictionary. They remain satisfied with the status quo and see no need for improvement. They believe in God, but possess no desire to tackle extraordinary feats for the kingdom of God. They hang on to yesterday's bread, even though it's stale. Caretakers lose pace with the world around them.

They see no need to stay on top of the latest advancements in technology. They live from day to day, with no projections for the future. When something breaks, they simply repair it. Why replace it?

Church as usual satisfies their low-level spiritual requirements. We have many caretakers in the Church. Some of them were saved beside the piano, located in the right corner of the church. That piano will stay in that exact spot until Jesus comes! Their uncle's father sat in the second pew of the middle section, right hand side, for 40 years. After he passed away, their uncle sat there for 20 years. That pew is now officially registered as a family heirloom. Woe to the outsider who sits there!

Caretakers, however, do have one redeeming quality. They are faithful to attend church. They may not be going anywhere, spiritually speaking, but they show up every time the doors are opened. They are oxymorons, the product of religious mind sets. If for some miracle, a new building is needed, caretakers offer no help. In their way of thinking, buildings cost too much money. The old building has served them well. Why break with traditions and old habits? Sadly, the work of the Lord suffers at the hands of caretakers.

Risk Takers

This group ushers a fresh move into the Church. Among their ranks you find faith and excitement. These are the visionaries. They love the anointing, and their spiritual eyes are open. Risk takers, like Peter, are willing to get out of the boat, and to forge past their comfort zones.

The spirit of a risk taker compels him to attempt what others have never tried.

He sees things in the Spirit, things that move him beyond the possibility of even a good example. Thank God for good examples. We need good examples to follow. However, a risk taker blazes his own trail; while the undertakers and caretakers stand alongside the road and criticize.

Risk takers are not irresponsible and reckless; they move in faith. They are, however, willing to leave the safety and security of the boat in order to walk toward uncertain waters. Peter may have sunk, but at least he stepped out of the boat! He did sink, but he also walked. Even undertakers and caretakers have to admit that Peter, the risk taker, accomplished something purposeful.

The first two groups of people always stay in the boat; they never attempt anything risky, and they never walk on water. Perhaps you are never criticized. Check your pulse! Understand, if you do nothing for God, you will accomplish nothing of eternal value. Usually, only those who attempt great feats for God meet up with the critics.

I CHOOSE TO GET OUT OF THE BOAT OF MY COMFORT AND SINK IN THE WATER, IF NECESSARY. I WANT TO BE A RISK TAKER FOR GOD. I MAY BE CRITICIZED, BUT AT LEAST IT WILL BE SAID THAT I TRIED!

Risk takers are not show-offs; they live to bring glory to God. Their motivation, despite what their critics may say, is to see the glory of God.

Paul too, was a risk taker. He was transformed from Saul into Paul. He moved from ambition to vision. He was a self-appointed religious zealot, who embraced a God-appointed ministry. What people said about him, no longer affected him. Popular opinion would not sway the man from Tarsus. Imagine what the world would have missed had Peter, Paul and countless others refused to step into their destinies. Risk takers like these move in faith, and always catch the eye of God.

I love risk takers. The Old Testament talks about three other men (there are many others) who were willing to risk their lives to accomplish great feats for God.

Again, I'm reminded of Joshua and Caleb, two of twelve leaders that Moses sent to spy out the land. The group returned with their report. Ten of the men asked, "Did you see the size of those giants?" Joshua and Caleb said, "Yes, but did you see the size of those grapes?" Their eyes were fixed on the grapes of God's blessings, not on fear and unbelief.

Second, do you remember the young lad who took on the giant Goliath with only a sling and five smooth stones? Of course you do! The terror-stricken soldiers standing around the shepherd boy were saying, "Did you see the size of that Philistine?" David thought to himself, "Yes, I see his size, but have you forgotten the size of our God?" God has always had his risk takers!

I was ministering in a church three months after my arrival in the United States. God, by His grace, used me to prophesy over a lady. God showed me that she was involved in both the occult and drug worlds. "Lady," I said, God wants to set you free."

Until I spoke those words, the woman seemed to enjoy the service. Afterwards, her entire countenance changed and she became a totally different person. Three men had to restrain her, as she tried numerous times to kick me and the pastor. Thank God, they were strong men!

The woman then got a strange look in her eyes, turned her head to one side and spit at me. The people were both frightened and amazed. The Holy Spirit said to me, "The devil just confirmed that I, the Lord, want you to be in this nation." I felt honored that the Lord would speak to me in such a manner.

The bark of the enemy actually confirmed my assignment!

The enemies of Paul tried to assassinate him after his conversion. In actuality, what they did was confirm Paul's God-given appointment. Some times the devil would do well to back off!

Dear risk taker, God has promised to oversee His plan. He has promised protection in the midst of your difficulties.

Focused on God's Plan

The days following Paul's conversion were action-packed. His former Jewish friends hated him with the same passion with once they love him. Their goal was to see him dead, so they patrolled the city gates around the clock. Acts 9:25 tells us that *"the disciples took him by night, and let him down by the wall in a basket."* Thank God for people who are willing to protect His plan!

For the first time, Paul finds himself a fugitive from his own countrymen. This former religious assassin, who forced people to escape for their lives, now found himself running.

All things considered, I would rather find myself unpopular in the eyes of people for preaching the gospel, than to be popular with no godly covering.

In Matthew's gospel we read where God protected the birth of Jesus. When Herod heard that a king was being born, he became troubled. All of Jerusalem was stirred, too. Why? They knew that something was about to happen that would threaten the kingdom of darkness. God was about to invest His plan in a little baby. Jesus was God's plan! In Matthew 2:4, Herod inquires as to the location of the birth. Providentially, the wise men were directed another way.

Remember, God always protects His plan in us, but He is under no obligation to protect our ideas.

The resistance Paul received from the enemies of the gospel would not defeat him. As a matter of fact, it made him stronger. Without vision, resistance will break you and force you to give up. With vision, resistance will make you even more determined to accomplish the purpose and destiny to which you were called. A godly vision cannot be diverted.

Many missionaries have given their lives for their calling. Others have forfeited creature comforts to fulfill their vision.

Again, if you are not willing to die for your vision, how can you expect others to follow that vision? Paul ran his race with patience. Focused, dedicated and single-minded, he built the kingdom of God. He was highly productive and unstoppable. Those who hear a clear word from the Lord find the strength to go on, even when facing the most difficult obstacles.

The character of a man can be seen in what it takes to stop him.

Stop where you are. Go no further. Have you heard from the Lord? Do you have your marching orders? Are you going in the right direction? If not, spend time in His presence. Get His game plan for your life.

No one wants to do things for God, just for the sake of doing things. Even a short-term vision will accomplish more than a life time of aimlessness.

Trying to lead others without having a clear vision is an exercise in futility. Both you and your followers will be frustrated. Followers take on the characteristics of their leaders. Your visionless, frustrating spirit may come on them. Many times we accuse our followers of not being fresh and focused. Perhaps, they are emulating what they see!

One day a friend of mine told me that his church was going nowhere, due to a lack of vision. After much prayer, the pastor, who was an elderly gentleman, came to the leadership of the church. He was honest enough to admit that he had no vision for the church. He was ready to turn it over to another pastor. The Lord led the elders in making another pastoral selection, and within three months the church doubled in size. Thank God for a pastor who was honest and sincere enough to admit, "I have no vision. I am ready to move aside and make room for God's appointed man."

You cannot lift anybody higher than the level on which you find yourself. I cannot lead you into a place where I have not walked myself.

Effective leaders must first "walk it" before they can show others the way.

Vision allows us to remain one step ahead of those we lead, and vision always takes people to a higher level in God. Paul always stayed one step ahead. He kept his eyes fastened on the finish line. He paid the price to lead. Don't expect other people to pay the price for your vision. Jesus had to pay the price in order for us to experience the blessings of the cross.

John was one of several who stood at the cross beholding the suffering Savior. That was in A.D. 29. He would dedicate the rest of his life telling others about the One he loved. In A.D. 90, he beheld Jesus again. But this time, he saw the glorified Christ in eternity!

What John Saw on Patmos

Jeremiah, Isaiah, Elijah, Elisha and Paul were all changed by what they saw in the Spirit.

Next, we turn our attention to the Apostle John. He is the author of a wonderful dream-vision known as the "Revelation of Jesus Christ." Specifically, in chapter one the heading above verse 9 says, "Vision of the Son of Man."

Why does the Bible detail this man's experience? John saw Jesus in a vision. *"I was in the Spirit on the Lord's Day, and I heard behind me a loud voice, as of a trumpet, saying, I am the Alpha and the Omega, the First and the Last..." (Revelation 1:10).*

John says, *"I was in the Spirit..."* What a significant statement! Is this a place for only the spiritually elite? A thousand times "no." John was God's chosen instrument and scribe to pen the things that he saw; just as you are God's chosen vessel to accomplish other kingdom tasks. I assure you, that John was overwhelmed by what he saw.

Here was a man, while living in the natural world, was granted a long look into the spiritual world. John's glimpse into eternity transcended the fact that he was exiled on the Isle of Patmos. He was caught up in a dream-vision of the One who had ascended back into heaven almost 70 years prior.

John, now at 90 years of age, was given a panoramic view of Jesus Christ in eternity. However, this time, His Savior *"had hair as white like wool, eyes like as a flame of fire, and feet like unto fine brass" (1:14 and 15).* John must have compared Jesus to how He looked when He walked with His Master seven decades before. The apostle outlived the original band of Twelve, who so closely walked with Jesus for three and one-half years. This aged apostle could walk, move, see and function in a world apart from his natural world – the world of the Spirit. At that moment the spiritual world was even more real to John than his natural surroundings. *"I was in the Spirit on the Lord's day..." (verse 10).* What an incredible experience!

God clearly instructed John to write the things that he saw in a book and send it to seven churches in Asia Minor. Notice, God did not tell him to write the things he heard, but rather, the things he saw (verse 19). John the Beloved, who previously heard a familiar voice, was later given the ability to see in the Spirit. He both heard and saw! While hearing the voice of God was wonderful, John's ability to see in the Spirit brought the world a much deeper, clearer and more impressive revelation.

Remember, John first heard a voice. Samuel, as a little boy, heard a voice. Jeremiah heard a voice. Paul heard a voice. Billions throughout the ages have heard the voice of God. But then John went further. *"And I turned to see the voice that spoke with me" (verse 12).* John heard the voice of Jesus and turned to see His face! He encountered a face-to-face relationship. He "turned" to see.

Every voice has a face!

The face plays an important role in terms of fellowship and relationship. John heard the Master's voice and then saw His face.

We too, need to see the face of God – more than ever before. Of course, in our natural body we cannot take in His full glory and stand. But hunger for God drives us to seek His face.

When I hear the voice of my only daughter, I desire to look into her beautiful blue eyes and see her face. Thank God that we can hear His voice, but the main goal in our relationship with Him should be to see His face. John turned and saw Jesus!

"To turn" means to exchange our present focus for something better.

John then said, *"And being turned; I saw seven golden candlesticks" (verse 12).* These seven lamp stands represent the Church – the perfect Church. Seven is God's perfect number. What God shows us in the Spirit is perfect. God showed John the Church. Jesus loves His Church! His heart yearns for His people. To know and love the Church as God does, requires that we see her in the Spirit. God does not show us things of no value, only those things that are precious to Him.

Verse 13 relates that in the middle of these seven lamp stands, John saw *"One like the Son of Man."* Hallelujah! His heart must have raced, as he beheld His wonderful Lord!

As a young man, John was one of three who walked in the inner circle with Jesus. If you recall, it was John who laid his head on Jesus' bosom during the Passover meal the evening before the Lord's crucifixion. You have heard it said, "Follow your heart." John's heart always took him to the Master.

Jesus was seen in the midst of the seven lamp stands. The word “midst” means middle. He will always be found in the middle of His Church. The presence of God is the same world-over. He is not more present in America than He is in China or Africa. God has the divine ability to live in the middle of His whole Church at the same time. He simultaneously works in China, while giving His attention to the Church in Africa. He never books the American Church for a later time; He is in the midst of His Church universal. The Holy Spirit works in the world-wide Church 7-24-365! And during leap year, too! He has promised to always be with us, His Church.

In verses 13-16, John describes the Lord’s garment and physical features. What made it possible for John to be so specific? There are no shadows in the Spirit world. John saw clearly! When you see in the Spirit, God shows you details.

More than once I have heard stories of those who briefly went to be with the Lord and then came back to earth. They gave detailed accounts of heaven and described to perfection what they saw.

Make no mistake, John saw in the Spirit. He saw the glorified Jesus. His description was accurately detailed. His dream-vision exalted Jesus and Jesus alone. Upon seeing the Lord, he fell at His feet. I wonder how we will respond when we first behold Jesus in eternity?

He Saw and Fell

As mentioned earlier, you cannot receive a vision of the Lord and not be changed. This cannot be overstated.

A vision that does not change the one who saw it, was probably not a true glimpse into the supernatural realm.

John records, *"And when I saw Him, I fell at His feet as dead" (Revelation 1:17).* Flesh cannot look into the supernatural realm and not be changed. John saw and fell down. Time did not allow for a committee meeting to discuss whether it was biblical or not to fall down. These issues are of little significance when we see in the Spirit. John *"fell at His feet as dead."* These words are of great importance.

Dead people care not what happens to them. Dead people don't feel it when they hit the floor. John said he went down as dead. He responded to the awesome holiness of God by falling at His feet.

When you encounter the Giver of life, your flesh has no choice but to die.

Our life is in Him. He is life! To worship Him is to acknowledge His attributes. To fall as "dead" before Him demonstrates paradoxically, that we acknowledge Him as life. Jesus said, *"I am the Way, the Truth, and the Life" (John 14:6).*

Saul, who became Paul, earlier testified that he had to die in order to live. He would go on to write that wonderful treatise on the righteousness of God that we know as the book of Romans. Paul emphatically declared, *"We are the righteousness of God" (Romans 3:22).*

According to Paul, we have been set free from sin and have become the sons of God. The imputed righteousness of Jesus Christ both instantaneously and progressively sets us free from our sinful condition. We are no longer to be conformed to this world, but transformed by the renewing of our mind. We are not beggars any more.

God is holy. He is our Father and friend. Jesus is our elder brother, but He's not our play-mate. He's more than a "good ole' boy. He's not just your buddy from down the street. He supercedes our presidents and prime ministers. He is Almighty God! He is Jesus, Who stands in the middle of the lamp stands. He is your righteousness. Your fleshly desires must bow at His feet. Sin dies in the presence of a holy God. Ask Isaiah.

Read John's description. He openly admits, *"I fell..."* Let your flesh diminish and let God be exalted!

We must understand the difference between fear and reverence. John fell at Jesus' feet out of reverence, not fear. The apostle had loved Jesus from his youth. Most Bible scholars believe that John was in his late teens when he first met the Lord.

Seeing in the Spirit as John did, necessitated a close relationship with the Lord. Upon seeing the glorified Christ, a holy and reverential fear came over John. He trembled in His presence.

Countless times we read in the Word, "Do not be afraid." Or "fear not." God does not want us to be afraid of Him. He wants us to enjoy Him. He yearns that we draw close to Him. Walking with Him is not a scary thing. Walking in the Spirit and seeing into another realm will daily enrich your life. You will become a more fruitful believer as you allow Him to develop your spiritual eyesight. The threats of the enemy will appear much less destructive as you learn to see things in a different light. God wants to bless you with "eyes to see." Let Him touch you today! Don't fall prey to the "grasshopper complex!"

Do You See Grasshoppers or Grapes?

How you view your future correlates with your ability to see in the Spirit. Do you see grasshoppers or grapes?

To understand this question, read Numbers 13:2. God commands Moses, *"Send men to spy out the land of Canaan, which I am giving to the children of Israel; from each tribe of their fathers you shall send a man, every one a leader among them."*

God wanted these spies to check out their intended blessing! Canaan was their specific land of promise. He first wanted them to take a look.

God has blessings waiting in your future, too. Through the eyes of the Spirit you can look into your future blessings and begin to thank God for them today. The children of Israel had not yet conquered Canaan, but in the Spirit it already belonged to them. When we have eyes to see in the Spirit, we can *"call those things that be not as though they were" (Romans 4:17b).*

When the twelve spies returned, they issued this report: *"...It truly flows with milk and honey, and this is its fruit. Nevertheless the people who dwell in the land are strong; the cities are fortified and very large; moreover we saw the descendants of Anak there" (Numbers 13:27).*

They continued with their negative report in verse 31: *"...We are not able to go up against the people, for they are stronger than we."*

The clincher came in verse 33: *"...There we saw the giants (the descendants of Anak came from the giants); and we were like grasshoppers in our own sight, and so we were in their sight."*

The outcome of the report is recorded in Numbers 14:1, *"So all the congregation lifted up their voices and cried, and the people wept that night."*

All of the spies, except for Joshua and Caleb, embraced the "grasshopper complex." They influenced the camp of Israel to accept defeat. The Israelites saw themselves as grasshoppers.

"Not only are we grasshoppers," they said, "but our enemies think we're grasshoppers, too." God's people did not see themselves as victors, but as victims. Because of their failure to see themselves as God did, they missed out on the promises of God. They forfeited the Promised Land.

Tears and regret await those who choose to operate in unbelief and who refuse to accept God's best in their lives.

Caleb quieted the people in verse 30, and openly proclaimed his faith. If he were alive today, He'd be a pastor's best friend. He said, *"...Let us go up at once, and possess it, for we are well able to overcome it."*

He reminded them of the huge cluster of grapes they found, along with the plentiful pomegranates and figs. These grapes were found in the valley of the giants by the brook called Eshcol. He chose to report on the size of the grapes instead of the giants.

In every promise of God there comes a valley. But in every valley there is a cluster of grapes.

Perspective comes from the way we see, the way

we choose to look at things. Compare Joshua and Caleb's perspective to that of the other ten spies. Ten of the spies chose to think like grasshoppers, believe like grasshoppers, and act like grasshoppers. They missed an opportunity for God to demonstrate His power!

By the way, grasshoppers don't even eat grapes! Do not live like the ten negative spies. Open your eyes of faith and see God's opportunities for you. He has destined you to take your land of Canaan.

God was impressed with Caleb's resolve. He said, *"But my servant Caleb, because He has a different spirit in him and has followed Me fully, I will bring into the land where he went, and his descendants shall inherit it" (verse 24).*

Seeing through the eye of the Spirit today will benefit your descendants. Isn't that a sobering thought?

Only Joshua and Caleb inherited land that was promised to every tribe in Israel. They saw something that their fellow Israelites chose to ignore.

Visionless churches produce cry babies. They miss God's best. God's promises are thwarted because they choose to look at their future through the eyes of a grasshopper. How sad. We, who were created in the image of God, need not embrace a grasshopper mentality. We were created for higher purposes.

Just because the devil forfeited his original purpose, does not mean that we have to take on his attributes. No grasshopper complex for those who see in the Spirit! Go ahead. Let the Holy Spirit position you. Go for the grapes!

God has given you the ability to see through His

eyes. He's given you a *"future and a hope" (Jeremiah 29:11b).* Let Him touch you as He touched Jeremiah, Isaiah, Elijah, Elisha, Paul, John and many other God-appointed, vision-driven, risk-taking, history-making leaders throughout the ages.

Position yourself to hear these wonderful words, "YOU HAVE SEEN WELL."

About the Author

André van Zyl, a native of South Africa, has been in full time ministry for more than 23 years, along with his wife, Naomi. They are the parents of one daughter, Amoré.

In the early years of his ministry, André was appointed as national youth director and organized several major stadium outreaches across denominational boundaries. He still travels to South Africa on a regular basis to minister to the people who remain close to his heart. Presently, he is launching *Asuza Fire Conferences* and plays a key role in the church world in South Africa.

In addition, he has ministered extensively in several other countries and nations around the globe including Australia, Hong Kong, India, New Zealand, Suriname, Scotland and the United States of America.

Presently, the Lord is using André in a wonderful way in the States. The family recently moved their ministry offices **(Good News to the Nations)** to Atlanta, Georgia, from where they plan to minister to the continental United States. His love for the American people is obvious, and André receives many invitations to return to churches where he has previously ministered.

God has given André a very strong and prophetic word to the Church, and miracles, deliverances, healings and other signs accompany his ministry. God frequently uses André in the gifts of the Holy Spirit with much fruit. Because of his anointing, churches are corporately uniting to fulfill their purpose in these end times.

He has proven himself a worthy and respected leader in Pentecostal and Charismatic circles. He possesses a clearly defined destiny in Christ, and seeks to help position ordinary people and local churches to reach their full potential and destiny. Pastor André van Zyl is a father to many pastors and leaders in the kingdom of God.

Check out these other ministry resources from André van Zyl:

Single Audio Messages

Rebuilding the Kingdom Wall

God wants to rebuild the "broken-down walls" in your life. André draws parallels from the life of Nehemiah to help you in your reconstruction process.

The Life of Jacob

Jacob wrestled with God all night. "I'll not let you go unless you bless me!" he said. We, too, can determine when God stays or goes, not only in our worship services, but in the circumstances of our daily lives.

Unity

The psalmist says that God commands His blessings when the brethren live together in unity. What is unity? It is spelled, *"You and I Tie."* Jesus is bringing a new harmony back into His Church. Jesus prayed for unity in John 17, and Acts 2 says the early disciples were in one accord. With unity comes an increased anointing. A new river of glory is coming down. Jump in!

The Midwife Church

God works in seasons, and is about to birth a fresh plan in the Church. Like always, the devil is trying to kill God's plan. Pharaoh commanded the midwives to kill the new Hebrew males. Because the midwives feared God, Moses' life was spared, and the plan of God continued. God still protects His plan today. Can He depend upon you like He did the midwives?

God to Pharaoh

We live in a "pharaoh system," a worldly system. Just as Moses was a representative of God to Pharaoh in Exodus 7, we represent God to this world. Learn about the awesome responsibilities that God has placed upon us.

The Thronging Church

In Mark 5:28, the hemorrhaging woman said, *"If only I can touch His clothes."* In desperation, she pressed through the thronging crowd, and her faith made her whole. Today, Jesus is longing for individuals to move beyond the business of church activity. Many are "thronging" Him, but they lack purpose and intimacy with Him.

Count It All Joy

Is your life full of difficulties and temptations? Be happy, for when the way is rough, your patience has time to grow. Certain characteristics in our lives will never develop apart from trials and temptations. So, count it all joy! In this message, André shares how one leads to the other.

Compassion for the People

The parable of the Good Samaritan sets the stage for this message. The wounded man is a type of the Church. The priest is a type of a spirit; the Levite is a type of a "Pentecostal spirit." The Good Samaritan is a type of Jesus. Where are you spiritually? Find out!

A Holy Man of God

The Shunamite woman is a type of the Church, while Elisha is a type of the Holy Spirit. She said, "I know this is a holy man of God." By implication, she was saying, "This is more than just another move of God; it is a supernatural move of God." Do you hunger for a supernatural move of God in your life? This message will encourage you.

Is It a Ghost?

The disciples were in the boat, and saw someone walking on the water. "Is it a ghost?" they wondered? Jesus answered, "It is I." Peter asked another doubt-filled question, "If it is…" The boat represents the disciples' lifestyle. Jesus was walking on their trouble—the raging sea. God always shows up at a time and in a way we don't expect!

Married to Leah

Leah represents "reality." Jacob's dream was for Rachel. Remember, there's a difference between our dreams, and where we actually are. Reality is never what we want; our dreams are perfect. The key is that we stay where we are, learn the lessons that God has for us, and the dream that we love will come to pass!

Unwrap the Resurrection Power

We have an angry Jesus in John 11. He was not satisfied with the status quo. When He went to the tomb of Lazarus, He had something up His sleeve. He had deep feelings. Just as the grave clothes of Lazarus were unwrapped, Jesus wants to bring resurrection power into the dead areas of our lives.

Trophies of Christ's Victory

We are "trophies." God causes us to be triumphant. Jesus triumphed on "that cross," and made a fool out of the devil. Because of that wonderful victory, He leads us in a victory march, too!

See Into the Supernatural

Isaiah saw the glory of God. We, too, need to open our "spiritual eyes" to see in the Spirit. The prophet was not perfect, but he still tapped into the supernatural. He was aware of his own weakness—"Woe is me." Perfection (Jesus) opens the eyes of imperfection (us) when we submit our weaknesses to Him.

Audio Sets

Healings and Miracles

Andre says, "You get what you preach. If you preach 'miracles,' you get miracles." Let this 5-tape series stir your faith to believe God for your miracle!

The Glory Cloud

The glory of God is not goose bumps. His glory comes to those who are hungry. Miracles, signs and wonders occur when people walk into the "atmosphere of God" where His glory abides. *"As surely as I live, and as surely as the glory of the Lord fills the whole earth..."(NIV)* Get under the glory cloud!

Blessed By God

Believers everywhere pray, "God bless me," just as Jacob did in Genesis 32. When wrestling, someone wins and someone loses. Even though Jacob lost, he won. To gain in the Spirit, you must lose in the flesh. You, too, will win when you lose to God.

Arise, Shine!

Arise, Shine—two commands that must take place in that order. When you obey, *"the glory of the Lord will be risen upon you."* Some believers and churches may shine, but their light is dim. They must first be positioned to go forth. Isaiah 60 reveals the *kabod*, or "weightiness of God" that comes upon you. And then the glory of the Lord will shine forth!

Miracles in a Deserted Place

We're living in the last days, and time is wearing away. Sadly, many are not in the position to receive miracles. The disciples unanimously asked Jesus to send the crowds away in Luke 9 because it was a deserted place. But Jesus never sends people away. When everyone has deserted you, *He is the majority*. He will make a way for you!

Dead Things Live Again

The world says, "We are lost. We are dead. We have no hope." But the Lord says otherwise through His prophet, Ezekiel. He speaks to the dry bones and the dead live again! This "death valley" symbolized the spiritual condition of national Israel. Just as God breathed live back into those dead corpses, He wants to breathe into your life. We decorate death, but Jesus raises people from the dead through His power. You, too, can walk out of the valley of death.

The Holy Spirit

In order to receive the fullness of what we can get from God, we must move into the realm of the

Spirit. This seven-tape series explores the person and work of the Holy Spirit, as He operates through the five-fold ministry and gifts He has given to the Church. This is a "must" series for the believer who wants to become intimate with the Holy Spirit.

The Bud of Promise

No work is good until it's completed. Paul said to the Philippians, *"I want you to be confident that He who began a good work in you will complete it."* What God starts in us is good, and people will be attracted to it. The anointing makes you attractive. In this series, André teaches that anything God starts in us is like a "bud filled with promise."

For ordering information,
call (770) 271-4421,
e-mail: gnninfo@aol.com
or log on to the ministry website at
www.gnni.org.

Look for new audio messages and books!

FINISH READING
NOVEMBER 6 11:11 PM (ALMOST MIDNIGHT)
2005